AUTO DETAILING
For Show And Profit

David H. Jacobs, Jr.

Motorbooks International
Publishers & Wholesalers Inc
Osceola, Wisconsin 54020, USA

First published in 1986 by Motorbooks International
Publishers & Wholesalers Inc, PO Box 2, 729 Prospect
Avenue, Osceola, WI 54020 USA

Printed and bound in the United States of America

The information in this book is true and complete to the
best of our knowledge. All recommendations are made
without guarantee on the part of the author or
publisher, who also disclaim any liability incurred in
connection with the use of this data or specific details

Library of Congress Cataloging-in-Publication Data
Jacobs, David H.
   Auto detailing for show and profit.

   1. Automobiles—Cleaning.   I. Title.
TL152.J29   1986   629.28'722   86-12644
ISBN 0-87938-216-3 (soft)

*On the cover: 1985 Camaro Z-28 courtesy of Todd Dolan,
Polar Chevrolet, White Bear Lake, MN.*

Motorbooks International books are also available at
discounts in bulk quantity for industrial or sales-
promotional use. For details write to Special Sales
Manager at the Publisher's address

Contents

Acknowledgments

I want to thank the following people for their assistance during the course of work on this book: Dan Lux, owner of DJ's Detail, Lynnwood, Washington, and his crew, Scott Stanley, Steve Hoopes and Fred Wy.

Let me also thank the following people for use of their collector cars for the photographs: Joe Turk, owner of the 1968 Porsche 912 Targa; Gary Angell, owner of the 1967 Ford Mustang convertible; Gene Nordquist, owner of the 1957 Ford Thunderbird; and Craig Willey, owner of the 1965, 1976 and 1980 Corvettes.

I also want to thank John Blackburn and Van Nordquist of Gallery & Sons, Ltd. Photographic Studios, for the excellent job they did developing and processing the film and photographs.

Chapter 1

Detailing basics

Automobile detailing is a profession shared by men and women worldwide. Auto detailers make used cars look, feel and smell like new.

The most important phase in detailing is cleaning. Nothing can be dressed or painted unless dirt, grease and grime are removed. You wouldn't put on a three-piece suit without taking a shower, nor would you wax over a dirty floor. This same philosophy holds true for detailing automobiles.

Painting over a greasy engine might show a bit of improvement, but it would look tacky. There is no sense trying to make the engine compartment shine like new when there is so much grease you can't see the metal.

The same goes for the interior. Why spend a lot of money on deodorizers, when the cause of the odor is still in the car? If you transport pets, no air freshener will remove all of the dog and cat odor from the carpet and seats.

Detail shop with two Corvettes in line for the wash rack.

There are times when a thorough wash of the car's exterior will tremendously improve its looks. But exactly what is a "good" wash job? It is not simply running water over the body and drying it off. A thorough cleaning consists of scrubbing the tires and vinyl top, rinsing the fenderwells, removing bugs stuck to the grille and windshield, and much more.

When the dirt and grime are gone, a detailer can remove oxidized paint and get down to the layer of good paint. That's where the shine and depth are hiding. All other exterior washing will blend to complement the main body of the vehicle. Shiny tires, glossy black fenderwells, and bright chrome give an automobile that classic look. All areas work together for that fresh-from-the-factory quality.

Don't forget the trunk. Why have a compartment to hold all your incidentals, when every time you put something in it, it comes out stained and smelly? Detailing trunks does not take much time. A little vacuuming, elbow grease and clear lacquer paint can make it look new. You'll thank yourself later.

Importance of dirt removal

Besides appearance, there are a number of other reasons the engine and engine compartment should be thoroughly cleaned. Special heat-resistant engine paint will not stay on grease and grime. It might look good for a short time, but the grease will bleed through and ruin your attempts to make the engine look new again. Even if the paint sticks, the result will be a sloppy and unprofessional job. The texture will be rough and bad spots will be exaggerated.

Another reason for cleaning under the hood is to prevent rapid grease and grime build-up. Grease tends to collect more grease and oil. One spot of unnoticed oil will attract dust, dirt and more oil. Soon enough, you will find yourself cleaning the engine again. Speaking of

Painting over grease does not look good.

Regular engine maintenance is easiest on clean engines.

oil leaks, it is certainly easier to find them on a clean engine; repairs are easier, too.

Cleaning the engine compartment also gives you the chance to look for minor mechanical problems, such as loose wires or bolts, cracked hoses, bad electrical connections, missing screws and so on. These repairs may take only a few minutes, with the results guaranteeing a better running vehicle. They could even increase fuel economy, and we can all use help with that.

The interior of any automobile should look, smell and feel like new. A thorough vacuuming of the carpet will rid the passenger compartment of odor-causing debris, such as food, animal hair, candy wrappers, cigarette butts. A complete shampooing will remove stains, such as from spilled pop and coffee.

Carpet will last longer, too, with dirt and grit removed. Grit grinds against the fibers every time your foot touches the carpet. It is like a piece of sandpaper eating away at the texture of the carpet. Floor mats help, and I recommend their use, but there are always unprotected areas. Normal wear is unavoidable, but thorough cleaning will slow it.

Seats need to be vacuumed, too. You would be amazed at what can be found between them. Dirt accumulates in the cracks and crevices. Look between the bead of the seat and the cushion. Also, don't forget to vacuum the area at the bottom of the seatback and the rear of the cushion. This is the place where you may find pens, matchbooks, loose change and so on.

In addition to vacuuming, a good cleaning will remove the dirt and stains from the seats, and clean seats will not soil clothing. The grit

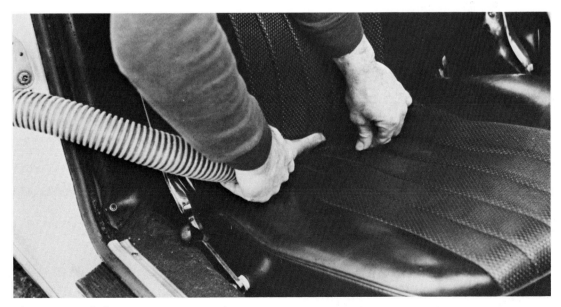

This is one of the most important places to vacuum.

and soil between you and the seat acts like a grinding agent. Shampooing will not prevent tears in the seams, but it will help reduce surface wear.

With a clean engine and interior, you will want a clean exterior too. A simple wash helps. But, if you want your car to look its best, you will have to give it a top-notch cleaning job.

Vinyl tops take a beating. They are flat surfaces which always face the sun. As the natural oils in the material dry, dirt can penetrate the top making it look old and worn. A clean vinyl top with an application of dressing looks and feels new. The dressing will also help protect the top against the sun and the elements.

Interior vinyl, especially the dash, takes much the same kind of beating as the vinyl top. Direct rays from the sun and the resulting heat dry the vinyl, leading to dirt penetration and cracks. Cleaning will help the appearance and prevent the soiling of clothes. Dressing will help protect it against the sun, and bring back the life of the material. Moisture and oils in the dressing should help prevent cracks. As with engine paint, interior vinyl dressing will exhibit its greatest luster when applied to a clean surface. (Make sure you read the directions on the dressing label before you use it.)

Most tires are black, although some appear brown because of imbedded dirt. It takes a cleanser, brush and some scrubbing to remove the dirt. Then, an application of exterior dressing will restore the tires' shine and luster.

Rinsing the fenderwells and undercarriage to remove caked dirt and road grime is also a good idea. (Paint will adhere more readily to the clean surfaces.) Besides enhancing the car's looks, reducing the amount of mud build-up might prevent future rust problems.

Buffing the paint is easier and more efficient on a clean surface. Buffing, or rubbing out, is hard work, especially if the paint is oxidized. Waxing alone will not remove tar or stains. The paint has to be cleaned first, using a mild liquid detergent or car-wash soap. For road tar, you might have to use a solvent-based chemical. (You can ruin a paint job by using the wrong chemicals to remove tar. So remember to read the label and follow the directions on any tar-removing product you use.)

Advantages of a complete detail

An automobile that looks, feels and smells like new is a pleasure to drive. It is no fun driving a car when your hands stick to the steering wheel. Nor is it fun going for a Sunday drive when you can't see out the windows, or when you have to leave them open to get a breath of fresh air. A complete detail will give your car the freshness it had when you first drove it off the lot.

With the skyrocketing prices of new cars, good used cars are maintaining high dollar values. There aren't many people around who can afford to trade in their used cars for new ones simply because they are tired of them. Most of us sell our old cars because they don't run right or because they look bad. So, when the time comes to change cars, your detailed used car will bring more bargaining power. Whether you trade in your car to a dealership as a down payment on a new one, or you sell it outright to a private party, your clean and shiny car will bring top dollar. How can anyone quibble on price when the product looks brand new?

Along with the cost of new cars, auto painting costs have risen, too. A good auto detail can save money in the long run. Paint will last much longer. A well-done wax job prolongs the life of the paint and sharpens the appearance of the vehicle.

Preventive maintenance is less work on a detailed car. When an oil leak is detected, it is easy to repair. Once the car is buffed, an occasional coat of wax will continue to protect the paint. The interior will need some attention, however, as time goes by. Its condition depends on you and your passengers; the more children you have, the more often you'll have to clean the interior.

Once a vehicle has been completely detailed, upkeep is much easier because the basics are done. A simple vacuuming normally keeps the carpets clean. Buffing the paint should be done only to remove oxidation or blemishes (the process actually removes a layer of paint). Simple waxing will protect the paint.

I believe a complete exterior detail might just help to increase fuel economy. An oxidized paint job feels rough to the touch, whereas a clean, waxed surface is smooth and slippery. A smoother surface should glide through the air easier. Although airplanes move much faster than the legal speed limits on the ground, pilots have told me that they have gained as much as twenty knots after a buff and wax. The same theory should hold for automobiles.

A clean engine should also run cooler. Without a coat of grease and dirt acting as a blanket, the powerplant should be more reactive to the cooling action of the air blowing by it. Moving engine parts on the outside, such as cables and linkages, should operate easier. This

Waxing is important. The removal of wax build-up makes the job look professional.

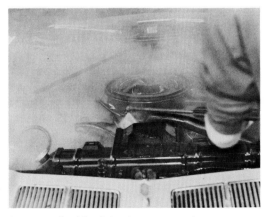

Remove the blanket of grease with a pressure washer and hot water.

includes the choke mechanism, which may be prevented from opening all the way because of grease build-up, causing the engine to burn richer than intended, a waste of fuel.

During the course of an auto detail, you will be using products and chemicals which could be potentially harmful to the automobile and detailer. It is imperative you read and follow the instructions on the labels of those products. No one but you can be responsible for the product usage; when applied correctly, the various cleaning, dressing and polishing agents will do an excellent job of helping your car look its best.

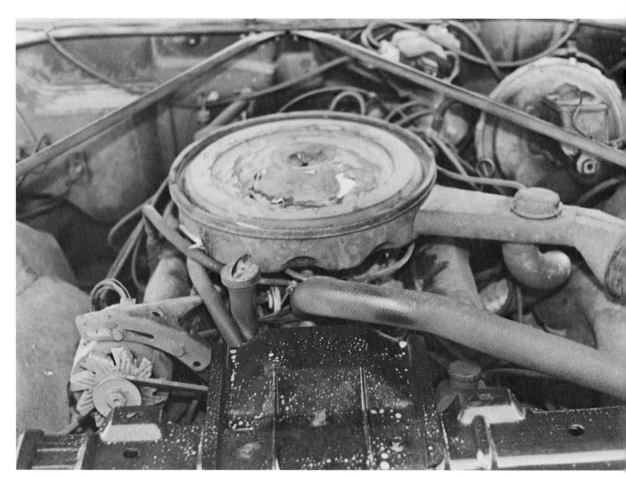

Dirty engines look as if they run rough.

Chapter 2

Tools and materials for cleaning

The tools and materials discussed in this chapter are things you will need to do a first-class wash job. Keep in mind that the tools and most of the cleansers you buy can be used more than once. The next time you clean your car, they will all be available. They work equally well on boats, motorcycles, 4x4s, campers and off-road vehicles.

Wash rack

To properly clean a vehicle, you need a suitable work area. A wash rack is any place where you can safely remove grease and dirt. In

Pressure washer, wet-and-dry vacuum, buckets, wash mitt, plastic brush, whitewall brush, cleansers and spray bottle.

the city, you can use the facilities of a self-service car wash. The two phases of a self-service unit include rinse and wash cycles. The rinse dispenses clear water, the wash also includes soap. This type of facility is ideal for cleaning engines. The only drawback may be the limited amount of time you can use the facilities.

Available in some areas are regular steam-cleaning facilities. Steam is an excellent cleaner, and it is a good setup for engine cleaning. As with the self-service car wash, it is equipped with drains for water, dirt and grease runoff.

If neither type of facility is convenient, try to find a spot with a gravel base. The rocks will allow water to run off so you do not end up with a huge mud puddle. Wash rack operations are crucial in detailing, and it is important you have a place where you can take the necessary time to clean your car and not have to worry about the mess. Any place will do, as long as you have water. Engine cleaning makes the biggest mess, so if you do not plan to do the engine, the wash rack area could be your driveway.

The wash rack phase of detailing is the most important part of the entire process. The initial cleaning of the engine, interior and exterior will determine, to a great degree, the ease, speed and final outcome of the job.

Degreaser

There are a number of commercial engine degreasers on the market. It's difficult to suggest or recommend one over the other. The

Frequent washings help keep an automobile in top shape.

best advice I can offer is to read the label on each product and choose the one which will suit your needs. Compare the different brands; the most expensive is not always the best.

Engine degreaser works best when applied through an aerosol can or a spray bottle. Either type will enable you to accurately spray the solvent. Advantages of a spray bottle are that when the contents are gone, you can refill it, and you don't have to worry about running out of aerosol propellant.

Petroleum-based solvents and kerosene are good degreasers. You should be able to purchase them in one-gallon cans. Auto parts stores, some gasoline service stations and some variety stores carry commercial engine degreasers. There are a variety of brands. Look for a product that cuts grease, road tar and oil. Read the label for cautions, and don't use a product that can destroy paint. This is important if any solvent should spill on top of the fenders.

Unfortunately, there are some ignorant people who use gasoline as a cleaner. *Never* use gasoline to clean anything. Used as a solvent, gasoline is a time bomb waiting to go off. I have read many newspaper accounts of people being badly burned or killed as a direct result of improper gasoline use.

Gasoline is extremely flammable. Its vapors are heavier than air and tend to stay close to the ground. The fumes may travel across floors and may be ignited by pilot lights on hot water heaters or gas dryers.

Water

Water straight from the garden hose generally produces enough pressure to rinse a dirty engine. A high-pressure unit works even

Wash rack area out of the way with all equipment in one spot.

better. Pressure washers are machines with an electric water pump, high-pressure hose and a special nozzle. Water from a garden hose is fed into the machine and the pump boosts the pressure. The resultant high-pressure spray is excellent for removing grease, dirt and grime. Used in conjunction with solvent, it takes no time at all to clean an engine.

Pressure washers are available at most rental shops. Their prices vary from place to place. In addition to engine cleaning, they are helpful in removing dirt from fenderwells and undercarriage, and from behind bodyside moldings.

If you don't plan to use a pressure washer or a self-service car wash to clean your engine, you might consider using a high-pressure nozzle on your garden hose. They are inexpensive and can be used for other things besides auto detailing. Local hardware stores usually carry an assortment of them.

Should you decide to use the garden hose, an ordinary nozzle will work. Be sure it is the type that will shut off immediately. Unnecessary water overspray will result in less control and a bigger mess.

Cleaning cloth

Cleaning cloths will be needed for a number of chores. The different portions of detailing require different textured cloths. Coarse cloths can be used for rough cleaning and soft ones for waxing and dressing. Rags can be used to clean wires and hoses. Soft bath towels work well on the body and the interior. Old cloth diapers are excellent for waxing. Before you start your detail, be sure to have plenty of cloths on hand.

Cleanser

Liquid cleansers are readily available at the supermarket. Chances are you have some already, perhaps under the kitchen sink. Any heavy-duty-strength multipurpose liquid cleanser is sufficient. It will be used throughout the cleaning process, from the engine compartment to the tires. The best way to apply the cleanser is through a hand-pump spray bottle. It enables you to spray the dirt directly and still cover a wide area. For other phases, you will need a small bucket of cleanser. You will add cleaning strength by dipping a brush into the bucket and then scrubbing.

Most multipurpose cleansers come in a refillable spray bottle. One large-size refill container should be enough for the whole job. Read the label to be sure the product you use is not harmful to paint or vinyl.

Special wheels, such as mags and chrome spokes, can be a headache to clean. Auto parts stores sell products designed especially for these types of wheel. As with most cosmetic car care products, there are a number of brands. Some kinds use a three-step method, others require only one.

Mag cleansers contain a small percentage of acid. The acid actually eats away the grime deposits, leaving the wheel with a nice shine.

Extreme care must be exercised when using an acid-based cleanser. Paint will not hold up to acid, so a thorough rinsing is imperative. Read the product labels to decide which will be best for you.

For most of us, clean windows on an automobile give a feeling of freshness. It even seems to make the vehicle run better. By the same token, smeared windows can make the entire rig feel dirty. That's why window cleaning is so important. Detailers spend a fair amount of time making sure all glass is perfectly clean inside and out.

A good glass cleanser with correct application can make short work of window cleaning. No special brand is needed. Just be certain it contains ammonia, which dissipates moisture and allows you to clean the windows with the least amount of rubbing.

Brush

Areas with heavy dirt build-up need more than just washing with a towel or wash mitt. An all-purpose plastic-bristled brush works very well. With sturdy, but non-scratching bristles, this type of brush will remove most dirt from engine, interior and some exterior parts. This type of brush has many different uses during a detail. It is available at supermarkets, variety stores and hardware outlets.

Whitewall tires require another kind of brush. For maximum whiteness, you should use a wire brush designed for scrubbing them. Spray the tire with liquid cleanser, then dip the brush in cleanser and scrub.

Special whitewall cleansers are available at auto parts stores. You can make your whitewalls or raised-white-letter tires look just like new.

Shampoo

Most auto upholstery requires no special shampoo. Any carpet or upholstery shampoo will do the job. Most supermarkets carry an assortment of these products. Read the labels and comparison shop.

High-pressure water from a pressure washer wand works well to remove grease, grime and dirt.

Use window cleaner and a clean towel.

15

The shampoo container will indicate the number of square feet it will cover. One quart should take care of normal shampooing needs. Exceptions are carpeted vans and campers; the more carpet to clean, the more shampoo is needed.

Auto shampooing does not require a special applicator. Pour the shampoo in a small bucket and dip in the plastic-bristled brush. The brush will absorb enough shampoo to cover a small area. That's how you do it, a small area at a time.

Car wash soap

Washing the exterior body of a car is a routine we all learned long ago. A good washing will not only make the car look good, it will make the job of buffing much easier. There are no special tools needed for this phase. All you need is a wash bucket, soft liquid detergent and a wash mitt.

Auto parts stores and some variety stores carry special car wash soaps. Read the label before you buy. Some products claim they help prevent the formation of water spots. Water spots are a hassle and anything that reduces them is a real plus.

Very soft liquid dish-washing soaps are best for washing cars. When you rub on a painted surface, anything hard can leave a scratch. Therefore, if a small grain of powdered soap did not dissolve, it too could scratch the surface. With a liquid, you don't have that potential problem. And by using very little soap, you won't be taxing the wax job either.

Air compressor

An air compressor is a piece of optional equipment that can be used to blow out trapped grime and help with interior cleaning. After spraying liquid cleanser directly into a vent, for example, air pressure can be used to blow out the dust and dirt. Without it, you would have to resort to using a screwdriver wrapped in a rag or a toothbrush to get the same result.

Air pressure also makes it easier to remove dust and dirt from that area between the windshield and the dash: Aim the air hose at one end and hold the vacuum hose at the other. Whatever is pushed out by the air pressure is sucked up by the vacuum.

If you have a compressor, you can also do much of the painting. If not, aerosol paint cans work very well.

Vacuum cleaner

To shampoo carpets, you will need a wet-and-dry vacuum cleaner. These units are powerful tools that make vacuuming easy. Ordinary vacuum cleaners will not pick up water. The wet-and-dry type must be used to remove shampoo from seats and carpet. If you don't own one, a unit can be rented. Self-service car washes usually have them near the wash rack.

For dry use inside the car, an ordinary vacuum with a hose attachment is the kind to use. The hose allows maneuvering and easy handling. Use the crevice tool at the end of the hose to get into hard-to-reach areas. It is easy to handle. Vigorous movement will break loose grit, hair, pieces of vegetation and so on. Although it may seem as if a bigger vacuum head would cover a broader area and speed the process, the crevice tool allows more concentrated suction. This results in a better job and doesn't take any longer.

The strong suction of the wet-and-dry vacuum also comes in handy for removing water overspray from carpets, seats, doorjambs and panels.

Decal and sap remover

If your car is covered with decals, and you have decided it's time to get rid of them, you'll need a razor scraper and possibly a liquid decal remover. The razor scraper is a common tool often used to remove paint from house windows. It works well to remove decals on chrome bumpers and glass. You can also use it on painted surfaces such as doorjambs.

Before using the razor scraper on painted surfaces, try one of the liquid decal removers available at the auto parts store. Too often the razor slips and takes paint along with the decal. The process is also very tedious.

Liquid decal removers are a special solvent designed to loosen the glue that holds the decals in place. By following the directions, you should be able to remove just about any decal.

Tree sap is also difficult to get off painted surfaces. Get advice from your local detailer. If the liquid formulas designed to remove sap don't work, you may have to use a razor scraper. Use extreme caution; the slightest error will scratch the paint. Hold the scraper so it is flat with the surface to be cleaned. Go very slowly. Do not try to get all the sap off in one swipe. Chip away at the sap a little at a time. When the bulk of sap is gone, use rubbing compound to remove any residue.

Chapter 3

Engine compartment cleaning

To clean the engine and engine compartment, you will need a degreaser (solvent), soap solution in a spray bottle, a plastic-bristled brush, an old wash mitt or towel and a water supply. A pressure washer works best, although a garden hose with nozzle will suffice.

You can clean the engine without covering the distributor, but it may get wet. Protect the distributor before spraying any water into the engine compartment. Take great care, the engine will be hot!

One way to do it is to place a piece of plastic over the entire distributor. Then, tightly tape the bottom. This will prevent water from entering the inside of the cap. The only drawbacks are that the distributor cannot be cleaned, and the plastic may melt on the hot engine.

Another way is to remove the distributor cap and place a piece of plastic over the points and rotor, then replace the cap. This will prevent water from getting on the points. Some water may get into the top of the cap, but when the engine is done you can dry it by using a soft, dry cloth. You can also use an air hose to blow it out. If you don't have an air compressor, you can use a hair blower. These blow dryers work very well. They blow out hot air at a reasonable pressure and can dry a distributor cap in no time.

A piece of plastic keeps the points dry.

Blow dryers work well to dry distributor caps.

Before you start to clean the engine, make sure it's hot. If you drive to a self-service car wash, the engine will already be warmed up. If not, allow the engine to warm up to operating temperature before beginning.

A warm engine helps loosen the grease. A lot of the grease can be blown off by water pressure without using degreasers. This makes the job easier and requires less solvent. The solvent-degreaser will also have better penetrating power on a warm engine.

Rinse compartment

Using water, spray the entire compartment except the hood. Try to remove as much grease and dirt as possible. Start at the firewall and work toward the front of the car.

A high-pressure line will remove most surface dirt. After the firewall, work on the top of the engine. Be sure to get the air-cleaner housing, manifold and rocker covers. Then, move down the side of the block reaching everything possible. After that, rinse the front of the block, watching for grease behind the alternator, power steering unit and so forth.

When you have completely rinsed the engine compartment, stop to take a look at what you have done. Look for any spots you missed. Try to clean missed areas again with just water pressure. Be sure to look over the front of the block. This is an area where little pockets of grease and dirt commonly hide.

Spray solvent on grease

Once the carburetor is covered and protected, spray it with solvent-degreaser. Let it soak in for a minute and then rinse. Continue until the carburetor is clean. Spray and rinse the intake manifold and rocker covers. Then spray the firewall and rinse. When you find a stubborn spot, use the plastic-bristled brush to scrub it clean.

Be systematic in your work; it promotes good coverage the first time around.

It is hard to clean the carburetor with the air cleaner in place.

19

Work in a set pattern. Start at the carburetor and the top of the engine. Then clean one side. Move on to the front of the block and be sure to spray all areas behind the alternator, power steering unit, air conditioning unit and so on. Use the scrub brush as necessary. Then, go to the other side of the engine to clean. Concentrate on the greasy areas of the engine. Stop periodically to check your work. Stick your head into the engine compartment and look for those out-of-the-way places.

Engine grease finds many places to hide. Some of the more commonly missed spots are located under and behind engine accessory parts. They include the brake fluid reservoir, the top of the bell housing, and around the water pump, power steering units, air conditioning parts and alternators. Stand to the side of the engine and check the back sides of these parts. (On 4x4s and some pickups, you may have to stand on a stool to get a good view of the engine.)

Look under the exhaust manifolds and next to the spark plugs. Here, the block accumulates lots of grease. Many water pumps have grooves in them which make grease removal difficult. Spray with

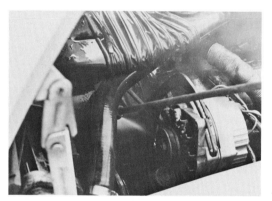
Wand from the pressure washer removes grease from the front of the engine.

Look in those out-of-the-way places for hidden grease.

Use plenty of solvent to loosen grease on the side of the engine.

Kneel on the hose to prevent your pants from getting wet and greasy while rinsing the undercarriage.

degreaser and scrub with the brush. Rinse and recheck. Many times you will have to go over a spot two or three times before it is completely clean.

The bottom parts of some very greasy engines need to be cleaned. You may have to do this from under the engine. Bend down in front of the vehicle and spray as much of the block as you can. Rinse it with water and recheck. This is not necessary on all rigs, just the really neglected ones.

Solvent and water pressure work very well together. You should not have to climb under the car to clean the bottom of the block.

Some of the special problems associated with auto detailing seem to refer back to the cleaning process. A few extra minutes spent removing grease from the engine will pay off later. And remember, the cleaner the engine, the easier it will be to paint.

Clean engine compartment

The engine compartment is either painted the same color as the car or it is black. After the engine grease has been removed, the next step is to use soap and water to clean down to that color. With a small plastic-bristled brush, a spray bottle of soap and an old wash mitt, you can thoroughly clean any engine compartment.

I also suggest using a small bucket filled with soap solution. Dip the brush into the bucket before each application. This gets even more cleaning solution on the surface.

Rinse the entire engine compartment with water. This will remove any loose dirt or grease that has been dislodged while cleaning the engine. Using a set pattern, start washing the painted parts.

Begin at the firewall. Spray soap on it. Then use the brush to scrub heavily soiled areas. Use the wash mitt for not-so-dirty and easily reached places. Continue to wash and rinse until that part of the firewall is done. Next, do the fenderwells. Spray, scrub and rinse. Use the brush as necessary. It will not scratch the paint and is excellent for reaching into the ridges, edges and corners of parts.

Use the plastic-bristled brush to scrub the firewall.

The plastic-bristled brush works very well to remove grease and dirt from odd-shaped parts.

Use the wash mitt with your hand completely inside. There are many sharp edges in the engine compartment. The mitt will protect your hand from scratches and cuts.

When the entire engine compartment is clean, look it over one more time. Look carefully for missed areas. Don't overlook the sides of the radiator and the area behind the grille. When you are satisfied with the job, you can move on to the hood.

Clean air-cleaner housing (not fuel injection)

Use the spray bottle of soap on the air-cleaner housing. Use an old wash mitt or towel to wash it. Rinse it off and then remove it from the engine. Set it in the sun to dry.

While the air-cleaning housing is removed, you will have to protect the carburetor. Gently stuff a rag into the throat of the carburetor. Be sure the rag covers the opening completely, so that no water can possibly enter.

Never spray water directly at the top of the carburetor. Water inside will cause the engine to run very rough and will make engine starting difficult. If the engine does start, it will run rough until all the moisture is gone.

To further protect the throat of the carburetor, use a plastic cover from a coffee can. Try to pick one big enough to cover the entire opening of the carburetor. Poke a hole in the middle of the cover. The stem coming out of the top of the carburetor for the air cleaner will fit into the hole on the lid. After you push a rag into the throat, push the lid down on top of it. The lid will not fully close on all carburetors. Those with parts sticking out of the top will prevent the lid from lying flat on the rim of the carburetor.

Clean the hood

By saving the hood for last, you won't have water dripping on your head while you clean the engine. Hoods are usually painted surfaces, so you will want to use the soap, wash mitt and brush. Rinse the hood with water and then spray a quarter of it with soap. Use the brush to scrub. Do a quarter section at a time to make sure the soap

Let soap soak in to cut dirt, grease and grime.

You can use the plastic-bristled brush to scrub the hood underside.

doesn't dry out, and so you can maintain an even coverage. Scrub and rinse until it is clean.

The brush works well on heavily soiled areas. Be sure to clean the sides of the hood. Be very careful not to cut your hand on the sharp metal edges along the seams. Again, the wash mitt is perfect for this cleaning job.

Final touches

When the water has stopped dripping from the hood, remove the rag from the carburetor. Make sure nothing is left inside the throat. Check to see that the linkages are in place.

Pop the distributor cap and gently dry the inside with a clean, dry cloth. Use an air hose or blow dryer if available. Check the points and the plate. Dry as necessary. Replace the cap and the air-cleaner housing. If any other engine parts were removed, replace them now.

Start the engine and let it idle to make sure it will run. If it doesn't, check the distributor for water.

Allow the engine to idle while you complete the rest of the cleaning process. By the time you have finished, the engine compartment will be dry and hot—perfect for painting.

Periodically check the engine temperature gauge. If the engine starts to overheat, take appropriate measures. This seldom happens, because the car has to idle only a short while. If you realize you are taking too long, turn it off. Let the engine idle for about twenty minutes and then turn it off. When you are about fifteen minutes away from completion, turn it back on. This will give you a warm engine to paint.

If you notice an odd smell after the engine warms up, it is probably evaporating degreaser residue. The smell should go away in just a

Towels on the fenders protect the paint from grease, solvent and degreaser.

few minutes. If it doesn't, you had better look under the hood for a different problem.

Special considerations

In some cases, you may want to detail the engine compartment and not the rest of the vehicle; for example, a rig with a fresh paint job. You will want to protect the fenders and the top of the car from grease or solvent.

To do this, you will need some large towels. Gently lay the clean towels on the fenders. Lightly spray water on them to add weight. This will help keep them in place. Put towels over the windshield and the painted surface directly at the bottom of the windshield. Spray them with water also.

Hood insulating material should not get wet. Water would add weight to the material and cause it to fall out of its brackets. Moreover, it would drip water and be a constant source of irritation while painting the engine.

Work around the insulation by aiming the water stream away from it. Wash the metal parts as necessary without wetting the insulation.

Never squirt water directly at a part when you are standing in front of it. Always try to aim from the side. This will reduce the

Use water spray to the side of the insulation material on hoods. The metal is the only part that needs to get wet.

Rinse the fender often when cleaning engines.

amount of unwanted overspray. Wear safety glasses if necessary. Petroleum products such as solvents and degreasers can cause severe eye irritation. Spraying water from an angle will reduce the possibility of residue ricochet into your face. Nevertheless, cleaning engines is dirty work. Be prepared to get dirty and wet.

Chrome parts can be cleaned, but don't worry about shining them until you have painted the engine. Use the plastic brush to remove heavy concentrations of grease or dirt.

Use caution around stickers and emblems. Those with engine specifications and vehicle information should remain on the rig for authenticity. High-pressure water sprayed directly on them may cause damage or their removal. If you use a pressure washer, keep the nozzle away from them and use a light spray.

When using a solvent or degreaser, rinse the fenders each time you rinse the engine. This will protect the paint from harsh chemical build-up which could damage the paint. You can also rinse the windshield and top of the car. You can never rinse too much!

Chapter 4

Interior cleaning

It takes time to thoroughly clean an interior. Before you begin, make sure the vehicle's heater works. It will be used to help dry the interior.

Door panel and armrest

Starting with the driver's door, open and spray the panel with water. This will remove pieces of loose lint, dust and dirt. Next, spray it with soap from the spray bottle. Dip the plastic brush in a bucket of soap and scrub the panel. This method is fast and efficient. After scrubbing, rinse with water. Hold the nozzle up and direct the spray downward at the panel and away from the interior. This will prevent as much water as possible from entering the passenger compartment.

Spray the doorjambs with water. On the hinged portion, use as much water as necessary to get rid of old leaves and dirt accumulated between the outer skin of the fender and the fenderwell. If heavy concentrations of grease are present, use solvent to remove them. Rinse with water.

Spray the jambs with soap and scrub with the brush and mitt. Dip the mitt and brush in the bucket of soap before each application. Rinse with water, occasionally rinsing the body around it to prevent soap spots.

Scrub vinyl door panels and armrests with the plastic brush, soap and water.

Clean the hinged doorjamb to remove grease, dirt and accumulation of leaves.

Wash the entire doorjamb—top, sides and bottom. Do this on the door as well as on the body. You may have to hold the water nozzle inside the car and aim outward to avoid getting water inside the car.

This is the time to remove old oil-change stickers and service stickers from the doorjamb. Use solvent to loosen the glue on the stickers and then gently peel them off. If you have to use a razor blade, be very careful. One slip will result in scratched paint.

If the door panel is equipped with an ashtray, take it out. Empty it and then wash it with water. Put it back when you've finished so that it is not misplaced.

Continue this process on all doors and jambs. Use the solvent for grease and the soap for dirt. Use the brush as needed for the vinyl and the mitt for painted parts.

If you use a pressure washer, do not hold the nozzle too close to the door panels. Some of the imitation chrome strips on door panels are plastic with a thin covering of chrome film. This film can peel off under high-pressure water.

Trunk

Trunks with carpet need only the deck lid edges cleaned. Use the soap spray and the wash mitt. Aim water away from the inside of the trunk. The carpet can be vacuumed later. When the edges are clean, close the lid.

If the trunk does not have carpeting and is very dirty, you can give

Scrub doorjambs with the brush.

High-pressure water helps to remove old service stickers. Notice that the detailer aims the water away from the inside of the car.

it the works: Remove everything from the trunk, including the spare tire. Locate the rubber plugs installed in the floor and remove them. If they are too tight for your fingers, use a screwdriver (but be careful not to poke a hole in the plug or to stab your hand).

Once the plugs are removed, rinse the trunk. Water should drain through the plug openings. Spray the trunk with soap and scrub with the brush and the wash mitt.

Use water sparingly. Many trunks have large wells on each side between the fender and the floor. These wells accumulate lots of water. If you have a wet-and-dry vacuum, use it to remove the water. Otherwise, use a towel to absorb the water and dry the well.

As you stand at the rear of the car and look into the trunk, you will notice a piece of thin cardboard located at the back of the rear seat. This partition protects the back side of the seat. Keep this area as dry as possible. If water should penetrate the cushion material of the seat, it would be very difficult to dry. Eventually, it could even mildew.

If the trunk is not very dirty, there is no need to remove the plugs. If it is dusty, use a damp towel to wipe it clean.

Pickup cab

Interior cleaning for pickup trucks is the same as for passenger cars and vans. Scrub the door panels and armrests, and clean the jambs. But if your pickup is a toy that frequently finds itself in the mud, or if it is used in construction, you'll have an interior that could be terribly dirty. In these cases, you might be able to wash the entire interior.

Pickup interiors with carpeting cannot be fully cleaned, because the carpet would be water damaged. But, if the heater works and the pickup has a vinyl floor mat, you can thoroughly clean it with soap and water as follows.

Rubber plug removed from the floor of a pickup truck interior.

You can completely clean the interior of extremely dirty trucks.

Remove the seat. Locate the rubber plugs in the floor, and remove them as described for trunks. Rinse the cab with water. Avoid spraying water directly on the dash and speakers. Remove as much dirt and dust as possible with the least amount of water.

Spray the cab with soap and use the wash mitt and brush to clean. Dip the brush into the bucket of soap before each use. Use the brush on the rubber molding around the rear window. You will be surprised to see how much dirt is removed. Use a towel to clean the dash.

Rinse the cab with water and use a towel to dry it as best you can. Then, turn on the heater full blast. Set it for defrost so hot air goes through the dash. This will help to dry any water that got into it.

Trucks with severely dirt caked dashes need special attention. In some cases, you can carefully rinse the dash with water spray. This will remove dust and dirt from vents and the steering wheel, and cracks around gauges and heater controls.

Start by lightly spraying soap on the dirty spots. Then, quickly pass a fine spray of water over them to avoid getting too much water into the dash. Stay completely away from the radio and speakers. Use this method on the parts of the dash that won't be damaged by water, such as vents, steering wheel, heater controls, plastic glove compartment and gauges.

Remember, this extensive interior cleaning is only necessary for extremely dirty pickup interiors equipped with vinyl mats, plugs and an operating heater.

Special considerations

After the interior has been cleaned, remove and empty the ashtrays. Use water spray to clean them, and set them in the sun to dry before you replace them.

Floor mats should be removed next. While in the car, they prevent water from getting on the carpet. Take them out of the car to rinse and scrub with soap and water.

Vinyl seats taken out of pickup trucks can be scrubbed also. Use soap, plastic brush and water. When clean, place the seat back in the truck. This way, the heater will help dry it, too.

These interior cleaning steps are designed to save time during a complete detail. Getting as much done as possible on the wash rack makes final interior detailing much easier.

Chapter 5

Exterior cleaning

Tires

Clean the tires first, so water doesn't splash onto a clean surface. This will also give the tires and wheels plenty of time to dry.

All tires need to be scrubbed with the plastic-bristled brush and a liquid cleanser. For heavily stained tires, you may have to use a powdered cleanser. There is no need to use tire black on them every time they get a little dirty; just spray the tire with soap, scrub and rinse.

To get whitewall tires and those with raised white letters clean, use a whitewall wire brush. If you don't have one, a steel wool soap pad can be used (SOS and Brillo pads work well).

The whitewall wire brush has very fine bristles closely meshed. The bristles are short and as strong as those on a wire brush you would use on rusty old car parts, for example. These brushes are available at auto parts stores and some variety stores. They are not expensive and will last a long time.

Clean the entire tire first, then concentrate on the whitewall. Spray the white part with soap or whitewall cleaner. Scrub with the wire brush. Rinse and repeat as necessary until the whitewall or raised white letters are clean.

Wash the tires first so you don't splash dirty water on a freshly washed body.

Use the wire brush and soap for whitewalls and raised white letters.

Ordinary multipurpose cleansers work well on most whitewalls. But on those with severe stains, you may need to use the extra strength of a whitewall cleaner, which is also available at auto parts stores and some variety stores. However, the real trick to getting the white parts of a tire clean is the wire brush.

Wheels and wheel covers

Painted rims and hubcaps simply need to be washed. Because of their design, rims are hard to clean with just the mitt. I have had good luck using the plastic-bristled brush on rims. The soft bristles don't scratch the paint and they reach spaces the mitt can't reach.

If you have just repainted the rims, don't use the brush (new paint needs time to fully cure), use a soft cloth. On chrome hubcaps use #00 steel wool and wax, or chrome cleaner.

Don't try to remove all of the dirt and grime at one time. Scrubbing and scrubbing on a dirty surface will cause small dirt particles and grit to grind against the surface. Instead, scrub and rinse. Then repeat the process until the wheel is clean.

Special wheels and wheel covers need special cleaning considerations. Mags and chrome wheels fade and become stained. Chrome spokes also require special cleaning techniques.

Mag and wire wheel cleaners contain an acid-based formula which gets to the heart of the cleaning problem. You must use extreme caution with these products. Follow the manufacturers' recommendations to the letter. If you don't, you may end up with damaged wheels.

Remember that most mag cleaners are good for chrome but are not recommended for polished aluminum wheels. The acid in the mag cleaners will clean the wheel but will destroy the highly polished surface.

Mag cleaners come in one-, two- and three-step formulas. Read the labels to choose the one that best suits your needs. After you wash

Acid-based mag and wheel cleaners can be applied with heavy-duty spray bottles. Follow directions on the label carefully.

Use the plastic brush to scrub dirty wheelwell edges.

the wheel with the mitt, use the mag cleaner as directed. The acid in the cleaner will remove the dirt and stains.

Spoked wheels are very difficult to clean. You can use a toothbrush or a product made for chrome spokes (which makes the job easier). This is basically the same type of product as the mag cleaner.

Some spoked wheel covers can be removed for cleaning. (They can even be put in a dishwasher.) The basic wheel behind the spokes is cleaned with the mitt. Later, it can be polished with #00 steel wool and wax.

Wheelwells

After you clean the tires and wheels, use the plastic brush on the edges of the wheelwells. Most show cars don't need this, nor do cars with newer paint. But regular drivers get a lot of dirt and grime thrown onto the edges of the wheelwells. The brush and soap will remove the dirt build-up and reveal the good paint underneath.

The inside of the wheelwells should be rinsed. You will probably notice that quite a bit of dirt is removed from them. Accumulations of dirt in these cracks and crevices contribute to the deterioration of body metal. During winter snow driving, it is very important to rinse these areas often. This will remove road salt deposits, which are the number-one cause of car body cancer.

Clean wheelwells will allow black paint to adhere better. During the final phase of the detail, you will be painting part of them with glossy black paint. Too much dirt on the surface will prevent good paint coverage.

Undercarriage

Rinsing the visible undercarriage is very important on pickups and 4x4s because it will get painted the same as the wheelwells. Dirt accumulations will hinder the painting process.

Visible undercarriage painting can really set off a rig. For that reason, you will want to rinse the visible frame, steering controls and bars, rear differential, fuel tank and so on.

Vinyl top

The porous nature of the vinyl top material lends itself to the trapping of dirt. The dirt accumulation is not generally noticed until it is substantial. To get rid of it, first spray the vinyl top with soap, then dip the plastic-bristled brush in the bucket of soap, and scrub.

Rinse thoroughly. If you use a pressure washer, hold the nozzle about five to six inches from the surface to allow water pressure to penetrate and remove dirt. Be very careful around edges and seams. High-pressure water could force open a piece of the vinyl.

I have found it best to scrub half of the top and rinse, then do the other half. Use the brush in a circular motion; first in a clockwise direction and then in a counterclockwise circle. Don't let the soap dry, especially on any painted part of the body.

For vinyl tops with extremely soiled vinyl, use a vinyl top cleaner available at auto parts stores. Chemicals in these cleaners are very potent, so you must follow the directions on the label.

In areas with wet winter climates, vinyl tops are susceptible to mildew, which looks like many very small spots on the surface. An example is cars that sit outside all the time and accumulate leaves and pine needles. The leaves and needles catch in the rain gutters of the top and mildew.

To remove mildew spots, use the brush and soap. If liquid cleanser is not strong enough, use a powdered cleanser with the brush.

Heavy cleaning and scrubbing of the vinyl top removes much of the natural oils in the material. After you clean the top, be prepared to dress it with vinyl top dressing.

Body

By this time, the motor has been idling for some twenty minutes. Check the temperature gauge to be sure there is no problem with overheating. The motor is idling to help dry the engine compartment. If you did not clean the engine compartment, there is no reason for the engine to idle while you clean the rest of the car. If your car is air cooled, you should check the owners manual to see if prolonged idling is harmful.

Begin with clean soapy water and a clean wash mitt to wash the body. If you used the bucket while scrubbing tires, dump it out and mix a fresh soap solution. (Small pieces of grit will have accumulated in the wash bucket and mitt. If they are not removed, they could scratch the paint.) It is a good idea to use two mitts—an old one for the engine compartment and wheels and a newer one for the vehicle body.

You need only a small amount (a capful) of mild liquid dish soap in the wash bucket. If you use a car-wash soap, follow the directions on the label.

There aren't many tricks to washing a car except to wash every square inch of the body. Wash a section and then rinse. Don't let soap

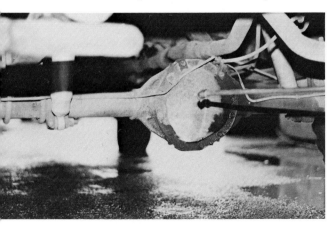

Pressure washer wand about to rinse rear axle and visible undercarriage.

Scrub vinyl top with the plastic brush and soap.

dry on the paint; it could cause cloudy paint spots. Be aware that the hood will be warm from the engine idling. Water and soap will dry quickly on it. And don't be afraid to rinse. You can never rinse too much.

While washing, be sure to reach the underside of the body. Areas under the doors are bombarded with road dirt and grime. Most people fail to reach down far enough to clean these areas.

If the body and/or the exposed frame part is very dirty, you may have to use the plastic brush.

While washing the rear of the car, look below the bumper. Newer imports have a bumper that sticks out past the body, leaving an area under it that should be cleaned. Use water spray to remove dirt caught in the rubber guards on each end of the bumper.

Grille

Most grillework is chrome, and its biggest cleaning problem is removing bugs that get stuck on it. The easiest way to remove them is with the plastic brush. Spray the grille, license plate and headlights with soap. Dip the brush in the soap bucket and scrub. Rinse and repeat as needed.

Spoilers under the front bumper also need to be washed. The wash mitt generally does a good job on them. For very dirty ones, use the plastic brush.

When vigorous brushing is done on painted surfaces, very thin swirls may appear. They are easily removed by buffing or waxing.

Road tar removal

Most tar spots can be buffed out, but it isn't the best procedure, because the tar may penetrate the buffing pad and create a bad spot in the pad. This could result in scratches. Paint thinner also works. Use a

Reach down low on the sides of the car. Rocker panels get very dirty from road grime thrown out by the tires.

You can use the plastic brush to scrub road grime from exposed frame members and rocker panels.

very small drop of it on a rag and rub off the tar. Then wash the spot with soap and water. Be sure to remove all traces of the thinner. The easiest way to remove tar is with a tar-removal product. Available at auto parts stores, these products loosen the tar for easy removal.

Drying

Use a very soft cloth or towel to dry the car. Some owners use only baby diapers bought from a diaper service, since diapers are cared for in a manner that ensures softness. Soft cloths reduce the chance of accidental scratching.

Others use soft terry towels, large bath towels or Turkish towels (which have rough, uncut pile). They absorb a lot of water and yet are soft enough to prevent scratching. Very few, if any, detailers use a chamois. It accumulates too much dirt and is difficult to clean completely.

Start drying the car at the top and work down. Don't forget to dry the wheels. It will take two or three towels to do a thorough job.

When drying the windshield, don't forget to dry the wipers. Raise the windshield wipers about an inch above the glass and let go. The snapping action will throw water off the blade and will keep stagnant water from dripping down the glass onto the body. It will also make window cleaning easier.

After drying, pull the vehicle into the garage or carport for the final work. Put the keys in your pocket so they don't get accidentally locked inside the car.

Use the brush to scrub brightwork on the grille.

Spoilers and areas under the front bumper also need to be cleaned.

Chapter 6

Tools and materials for finishing

Dressing
Interior

A clean vehicle interior is something to behold, especially if you have children. Simple cleaning will not always renew the shine and luster of factory fresh. To rejuvenate the vinyl parts of the passenger compartment, you'll need to use an interior vinyl dressing. These products are available in auto parts stores and variety stores.

Dressing will penetrate the vinyl and restore some of the elasticity and most of the shine. There are a few different types of dressings, so be sure to read the labels.

Vinyl Top

Vinyl tops are cleaned by scrubbing with a plastic brush and liquid cleanser. The shine and luster are restored with vinyl top dressing. This product should be applied to a clean towel and then rubbed on the surface. The dressing acts much like the interior dressing for interior vinyl. The difference is that exterior vinyl top dressing contains agents that will better penetrate the vinyl and afford much greater protection.

Vinyl top dressing comes in a liquid and is quite sticky. It is especially formulated for vinyl tops, and has no other useful purpose in detailing. The hard-shell finish protects the vinyl from the rays of the sun and the elements.

Some interior dressings can also be used on vinyl tops, but they don't provide the lasting quality of the special vinyl top dressings. However, they can be used on tires and other exterior vinyl. This type of dressing includes a solvent that penetrates and opens the pores of the vinyl. A silicone agent is then absorbed, which gives the vinyl or rubber the ability to breathe. This extends the life of the material and produces a nice shine.

Buffing and waxing
Buffer

Oxidized paint needs to be hand rubbed or buffed. By far, the easiest way to remove oxidation is by buffing. A buffer is a hand-held machine very similar to a sander or grinder. The rotating spindle turns a buffing pad, which rubs in wax and removes bad paint.

For the novice, I recommend a buffer of no more than 2300 rpm. (You can buy or rent them.) High revolutions per minute could result in damaged paint. Many professional detailers buff cars with machines producing only 1700 rpm.

Lightweight buffers are also available for sale or for rent. They do the same job as a heavy-duty model. It may take a little longer to complete the job, but the lightness of the tool makes it easier to handle. The slower rpm also reduce the chance of burns.

Although it may take longer than the bigger machine, it will still be faster than buffing by hand. If you have never buffed before and are unfamiliar with power hand tools, I recommend you rent one of the lightweight buffers.

This model is used in the same manner and with the same precautions as the other. Watch out for obstacles and ridges. Even the slower speed can rip out antennas and wiper blades. Be just as cautious around bumpers. Pads are often ruined when caught on an edge of the bumper.

Buffing pad

The pads used on the buffer are very important. The rougher cutting pad is used to remove oxidation and scratches. Generally, you'll need a cutting pad for vehicles that have been neglected for some time. For newer cars with good paint, use a softer finishing pad. It will remove most of the barely visible scratches and swirls. Remember that the pad should not come in contact with water. That would prevent it from doing its best job.

When you buff a dark-colored vehicle with a cutting pad, you will notice a big difference in the color and texture of the paint. In the sunshine you will see light scratches and swirls. The swirls are caused by the cutting pad. Buff the car again with a softer wax and the finishing pad. All of the swirls will disappear and the paint will look great.

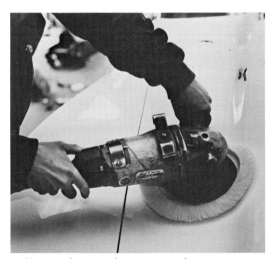

Buffer machine with cutting pad.

Getting the pad caught in the bumper may result in a tear. The pad will not be functional after that.

Buffing wax

Buffing paint with the pad alone will not remove oxidation or scratches. You must use a wax with it. Use a liquid or cream noncutting wax. The high rpm of the buffer negate the need for cutting wax on most finishes. (Cutter refers to the grit inside the buffing waxes. Rubbing compound has a lot of cutter in it.)

Cutting waxes are needed only on vehicles with extremely oxidized paint, the kind that comes off the car when you wash it. Using a wax with cutter in it increases the chance of burning the paint, which is when some of the paint is actually removed from the body down to the primer or the metal.

The best place to get the proper wax is at an automotive body shop equipment and supply store, which carries many different waxes with various amounts of cutter. The salespeople can help you choose the right wax.

Hand wax

After the oxidation and scratches have been buffed out, you should apply a coat of finish wax. I suggest using a liquid or cream. Apply the wax to a soft cloth and then dab it onto the vehicle. Squirting the wax on the paint first and then rubbing doesn't work as well.

There is no good reason to pack wax around emblems or in cracks and crevices. It makes removing the wax more difficult. Apply wax sparingly, as the directions indicate.

Choosing the brand of wax is up to you, but those with Carnuba wax as an ingredient are probably the best available. Use a wax with the greatest carnuba content. It will most likely be more expensive, but it will last longer and protect better.

#00 Steel wool

Chrome polishing requires #00 or finer steel wool, wax and elbow grease. Bumpers, mirrors, fender moldings and the like become lackluster after a while. The easiest way to clean the chrome is by dabbing a bit of wax onto a wad of #00 steel wool. This combination will rub off rust, dirt and overspray. The wax will act as a protectant against future build-ups, just as it does on paint.

Cutting pad on left, finishing pad on right.

Lightweight buffer with a two-sided buffing pad.

Special chrome polishes work equally well. They should be applied with a rag, however, not steel wool. You can use either method.

Nylon brush

Waxing the body and the chrome usually means some excess wax gets into areas that can't be reached by cleaning towels. Places like around emblems and light fixtures, in cracks between doors and fenders and in louvers.

Detailers get rid of that wax without removing the emblems or light fixtures. The secret is to use a one-inch-wide nylon paint brush. The nylon bristles are soft enough not to damage the paint, and the width is easy to maneuver. Longer bristles don't have the strength to remove wax, so cut them to about three quarters of an inch in length.

The short bristles have enough stability to withstand the pounding and twisting necessary to remove old wax. These handy little brushes can remove even the smallest particles and most stubborn wax build-up. By tapping the brush against the wax and twisting the handle at the same time, the wax is dislodged. The softness affords protection against scratching while the stoutness does the job.

Painting
Engine

If it wasn't worn off before you started, engine cleaning will remove some engine paint. Solvent and water pressure cause it to flake off, making a new painting desirable.

There are a variety of engine paint colors available at auto parts stores. Each spray can will have a label and a color-coordinated cap. The color you need depends on the make of the vehicle you are detailing. For example, General Motors products use GM blue, Chevrolet uses orange, Ford uses blue and green, and Chrysler uses Turbo blue.

Empty liquid soap dispensers work as well as plastic bottles for applying buffing wax.

Cut-off nylon paint brush works well to remove wax from the emblem of this 1980 Corvette.

Some International motors are red. Most imported cars come stock with no paint on the block or head. They must be cleaned and left unpainted. Before you purchase any paint, check under the hood to see what the original color of your engine was.

I recommend you use a stock engine color. Be sure the paint you use is made for engines. It is designed to stand up to the high temperatures created by engine operation.

Some parts of the block will require using the paint can upside-down. Since the stem of the nozzle extends to the bottom of the can, turning a half-full can upside-down will not allow the paint to reach the stem. For that reason, I suggest you buy two cans. This way, between the two cans, you will be sure to have enough paint.

Glossy black

Many parts in the engine compartment are black, such as the steering box, radiator, brackets, coil, voltage regulator and fenderwells. For these parts, use glossy black lacquer paint. Lacquer holds up well inside the engine compartment. The glossy nature gives a shine, where flat paints are rather dull. Glossy black lacquer paint will make your engine compartment sparkle, just as it did on the showroom floor.

Most engine-compartment painting requires just one can of black paint, but buy two. Then you'll have enough to paint the hood underside and other black painting as needed. Any leftover paint can be used later.

Clear lacquer

When the engine and engine compartment have been cleaned and painted, the overall appearance will have improved a great deal. The only eyesores will be aged wires, hoses and unreachable spots. This is where detailers have a secret. It is the use of crystal-clear lacquer paint.

Clear lacquer is available at auto parts stores and paint stores. In the can it looks like honey, thick and golden. Applied to a black surface, the results are amazing. It works on other colors too.

Hoses, wires, fenderwells and other parts shed their faded color and take on a new, fresh and shiny appearance. The clear paint will cover many dirt stains, water spots and some light oxidation under the hood. New cars are prepped with clear lacquer on the engine compartment. That's what helps give all those engine parts the shine.

In addition to the engine compartment, you can carefully spray it on vents, doorjambs, trunks, floor mats, metal beds (on Broncos and Blazers, for example) and many other metal and plastic surfaces needing a shine. One can is usually enough for one detail, but buy two. As with other paint, any left over can be used later.

On import cars with no paint on the block, clear lacquer is the only paint used under the hood. Be sure all the dirt and grease are removed before painting. Then, the clear lacquer will rejuvenate a rather dull-looking engine compartment.

Bright silver

Ashtrays lose their shiny silver finish quickly. Cleaning isn't always enough. Paint metal ashtrays with bright silver paint; plastic ones can be painted with the clear lacquer.

The bright silver color will give the ashtray a new look. Any overspray can be cleaned off with lacquer thinner. Use a rag to prevent overspray onto any painted surface on the front.

Bright silver paint can also be used on other parts such as radiator caps, air cleaner wing nuts and dock bumpers.

Paint block

Paint overspray is the biggest concern with engine painting. To prevent overspray and its problems, professional detailers use paint blocks, which are thin pieces of lightweight cardboard. Most of the time, I have used the license plate cards seen on brand-new automobiles. (These are the cards that fit into the license plate frame and exhibit the name of the dealer who sold the car.) The small piece of cardboard can fit into tight places and block paint from unwanted areas. For example, you could use a paint block in front of the carburetor while you paint the intake manifold. The manifold gets painted and the carburetor is protected.

A paint block can be cut out of a shoe box or any lightweight cardboard. An ideal size is similar to that of a normal license plate. It is easy to work with and affords adequate protection against overspray.

In addition to cardboard paint blocks, rags serve much the same purpose. A rag comes in handy when you want to cover an unusually shaped part such as an alternator or generator. The paint block and rags work well together.

Lacquer thinner

Don't get discouraged if you get paint overspray on engine parts, even though you use a paint block. Lacquer thinner will save the day! It's a must in all detail shops; even the professionals get paint on things they didn't intend to paint. Just dab a bit of thinner on a rag and wipe off any unwanted paint. It works great on hoses, wires, clamps and other metal parts.

Removing overspray from the engine is a true sign of a professional job. Nothing looks worse than a freshly painted engine block with wires and hoses covered in the same color. Stock is best and overspray certainly doesn't look stock.

Chapter 7

Interior finishing

It has been said that your automobile's interior is an extension of your personality. A sparkling clean and freshly scented interior will always express a positive feeling.

Vacuuming

A heavy-duty vacuum cleaner is the best type to use on auto interiors. The carpets in your automobile take much more abuse than the carpets in your home. Stepping from a wet parking lot or gravel road results in pieces of rock and grit in the carpet. The grit wears away the fibers and sinks deep into the pile. A strong suction is needed to remove it.

The best attachment to use is the crevice tool. With it, you can reach hard-to-get-at areas such as between the seat and seatback, folds in seat cushions, around the console, in the glovebox, under the seats and so on. Vigorous movement of the crevice tool gives the best results. As you vacuum, you can see grit pop out of the nap. Be sure the crevice tool is clean before you start using it.

The floor mats should have been scrubbed after the door panels and jambs were cleaned. Start this interior process by picking up all

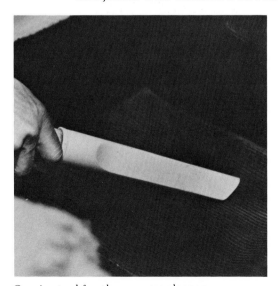

Crevice tool for the vacuum cleaner.

Use the crevice tool to vacuum around the bead of the seats.

the trash that has accumulated—candy wrappers, pop cans and miscellaneous papers. Vacuum the seats first. This way, any dislodged dirt will fall to the floor, the last part to be cleaned.

While you vacuum the seats, use the crevice tool to clean around buttons and seams, where lint and dust gathers. You can also use the crevice tool to vacuum tight areas between bucket seats.

For the carpets, start in the back and work forward. Be sure to push the front seat all the way to the front, then all the way to the rear, to be sure you reach the whole area under the seat. Begin at the middle of the car and work outward. Use brisk back-and-forth motions with the crevice tool. Do small sections at a time, covering every square inch of the carpet as best you can.

When one section has been completed, leave the hose in the car and walk around to the other side. This alleviates the need to move the vacuum cleaner. Most vacuum hoses are long enough to stretch from one side of the car to the other.

Continue vacuuming until there is no sign of grit popping out of the carpet. This may entail extensive rubbing and vacuuming, but it is the only way to ensure a complete vacuuming. Patting the carpet with the palm of your hand will release grit, popping it to the surface. This makes vacuuming a little easier.

Various vacuum attachments may work well on dusty carpets in custom vans. The crevice tool is still needed for sections surrounding pedestals and next to the paneling.

If the carpet in your trunk can be easily removed, take it out and shake it. Then, lay it on a flat surface to vacuum. This way is much easier than fighting with it while still inside the trunk.

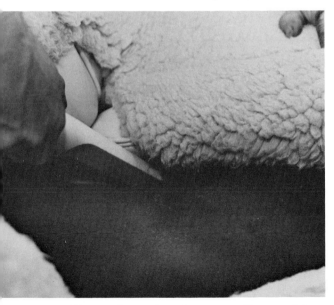

The crevice tool works very well to reach into tight spaces like those next to seats.

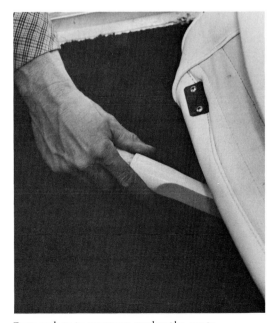

Remember to vacuum under the seats.

Wipedown

Every surface on the inside of the car has to be cleaned. Use the squirt bottle of multipurpose cleanser and a towel. Fold the towel into quarters for more manageability.

Spray the cleanser on one side of the towel. If the surface you are about to clean is heavily stained, spray cleanser directly on it. Then scrub it with the wet side of the towel. Use a dry side to pick up any remaining suds or streaks. Do small sections at a time, being careful not to poke a finger through the headliner or other covering. As the towel becomes soiled, unfold it to a clean side. Dampen it with cleanser and continue. Normally, one towel is enough for an interior.

Headliners subjected to tobacco smoke get heavily stained. You will notice a big difference after just one swipe of the towel. Continue cleaning until all stains are gone. Then, work down the sides of the interior, cleaning all the vinyl and metal parts. Clean everything in each section except the seat. Following that pattern ensures complete coverage.

For very tight places around the dash or center console, you can spray with cleanser and vacuum with the wet-and-dry vacuum. You can also use a toothbrush to scrub around knobs, moldings and vents. Wipe the gauge lenses with the damp side of the towel and remove moisture with the dry side. This will leave the lens clean and streak free.

The center console on bucket-seat models is cleaned much the same way as the dashboard. Use the toothbrush to reach corners and between cracks. Some people use screwdrivers inside the cleaning cloth to reach those spots. If you do, use caution; with excessive force, the tip of the screwdriver can poke through the towel and scratch any surface it touches.

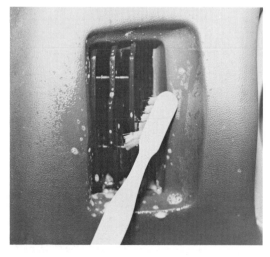

An old toothbrush works well to clean vents, knobs and cracks along the dashboard.

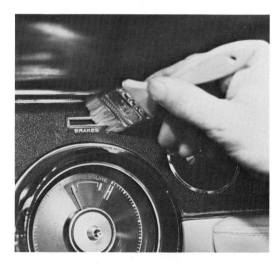

The cut-off nylon paint brush can be used to remove dust and lint in tight places.

Dusty dashboards and steering columns do not need to be scrubbed. You can use a corner of the towel to pick up dust around the gauges and steering wheel. If need be, you can use a toothbrush or the cutoff paint brush mentioned earlier. Either one works well to dislodge dust in the small spaces around dash fixtures. On the other hand, if the dash and steering wheel are very dirty and sticky, you can use the plastic-bristled brush to scrub them clean.

The glove compartment should also be cleaned. Use the towel to remove dust, dirt and remnants of things stored in it. Also clean the front side of the rearview mirror. Often, that side of the mirror is neglected. It isn't seen from inside the car, but is noticed from the outside.

Vents are difficult to clean. Since the openings are too small for your fingers, spray with cleanser and then use an air compressor or blow dryer to dry it out. The shaft of a screwdriver wrapped inside a towel, or a cotton swab, can also be used to clean the vents. Most of the time, the deflector shields are the only dirty parts of the vents. The dust accumulation is easily removed with the damp part of the cloth.

Vinyl seats are cleaned with soap and the scrub brush. Spray half of the rear seat with cleanser. Then dip the brush into the bucket of soap and start scrubbing. Use a towel to dry. Then, move on to the other half of the seat. Scrub the seatback first and then the cushion.

Vinyl seats are cleaned best when you use the plastic brush, soap and water.

The wet-and-dry vacuum can be used to dry around buttons and seams, but it is not mandatory.

When you have finished the rear seat section, reach forward and clean the back side of the front seat. You should try to clean everything within reach every time you start a section. This eliminates wasted motion and the need to keep hopping around the vehicle, cleaning here and there.

Vinyl seats that require lots of scrubbing will appear dull when dry. Multipurpose dressing will put life back into the vinyl and restore the shine.

Shampooing cloth seats

The process for shampooing cloth seats is very similar to scrubbing vinyl seats. You'll need the plastic brush, a small bucket of soap, the spray bottle of soap and a wet-and-dry vacuum. The vacuum is a must to remove shampoo from the material.

On some expensive cars, the seats are covered with unique material such as velvety crushed velour. If the upholstery shampoo you plan to use does not list it as a type of material it can clean, you may have to consult the owners manual or an upholstery shop to locate the right shampoo.

Generally, most cloth interiors consist of the same basic material used on most household furnishings. Upholstery shampoo available in most supermarkets should be capable of doing the job.

Start with the back seat. Spray the shampoo on the material and then dip the brush into a small bucket filled with the shampoo mix-

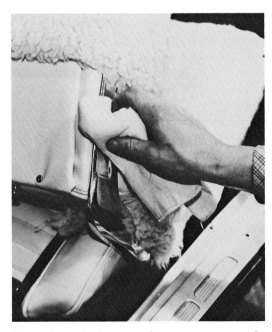

Use a clean cloth or towel to remove soapsuds and streaks from moldings and strips on seats.

Carpets are shampooed with the plastic brush, a spray bottle and a bucket of shampoo.

ture. Scrub the same way as described for vinyl seats. Work up a good lather.

While both the seatback and cushion are lathered up, use the wet-and-dry vacuum to remove the suds. Use the crevice tool, drawing it across the seat in a slow fashion. Allow the suction to pick up as much moisture as possible. When the lather is gone, vacuum the seat again to get every bit of shampoo that can be removed.

The seats will not be completely dry after vacuuming. It will take some time for the residual moisture to evaporate. To speed the process, you can park the finished car in the sun with the windows open. If it is a cool and cloudy day, you can let the car idle with the heater on and the windows opened slightly. Generally, on a warm day the seats and carpets dry by the time you complete the rest of the detail.

Dry the metal strips and moldings with a clean towel. If a stain persists, use a more concentrated shampoo solution or a stain remover. Be sure to follow the directions on the label.

Shampooing carpets

The same shampoo you used for the seats can be used for the carpet, which should be done after the seats. If you didn't shampoo the seats, then use one of the carpet shampoos available at the supermarket. Read the labels until you find the one that will work best for you.

The shampooing process is much the same as for cloth seats. Start in one section and work around the car. Spray the area with the spray bottle first, dip the brush in the bucket and then scrub. Vigorous scrubbing will bring up a good lather. When you finish a section, be sure to vacuum right away, removing as much shampoo as possible.

Grease and oil stains can be removed with spot removers. Some petroleum stains can be removed with solvent. Use caution when working with solvent. Too much solvent could damage the carpet by removing the dye in the fibers; you could bleach it out.

Apply the solvent to a rag, just a small spot is enough. Rub it on the stain, then shampoo as usual. Be ready to vacuum right away. Use the crevice tool to remove as much of the solvent as possible. If the stain has faded but not disappeared, try the same technique again. On the other hand, if it did nothing to the stain at all, you may have to seek professional help from a carpet cleaner or a detailer.

If your carpets are merely dusty, don't shampoo. If you want, you can even try a dry shampoo designed for household use. This may be the best way to go if you do not have access to a wet-and-dry vacuum. But, if you shampoo the carpets or the upholstery the way I have described, you must use a wet-and-dry vacuum, even if you have to go to a self-service car wash to do it.

Windows

Clean windows make an automobile feel clean all over. I'm sure you have noticed what a difference a clean windshield makes. Thorough glass cleaning is more than just a quick swipe with a chamois.

Use a good window-cleaning product with ammonia. Almost any brand will do. They are readily available at variety stores and supermarkets. You probably already have some that you use for the windows in your house.

Use a towel folded in quarters just as you did when cleaning the interior. Spray on the glass cleaner and wipe with one side of the towel. Turn the towel over to a dry side and pick up any remaining moisture and streaks.

Start with the driver's door window and work your way around the car. Be certain the car keys are out of the car. Too many times, door locks are depressed while window cleaning.

If seats are still wet from the shampoo, lay a clean towel on them. You should only have to do this to reach the back side windows on a two-door model, the insides of rear windows and the windshield. It is easiest to clean the windshield from the passenger side of the car, as you won't have the steering wheel in your way. Clean the rearview mirror, too.

As the towel becomes soiled, unfold it to a clean side. Exceptionally dirty glass may have to be cleaned more than once.

Dressing

Multipurpose dressings come in two basic formulas. The solvent-based type is good for interior and exterior work. I mostly use the water-based type on fine leather and rich interiors. Read the labels on the products to determine which is best for you.

For maximum results, dress every piece of vinyl inside the car. This includes the dashboard, door panels, seat belts, vinyl seats, foot pedals, floor mats and any vinyl in the trunk.

Use a clean, dry cloth. An old diaper or towel works fine. Fold the cloth into quarters, using only one side to start. Apply the dressing to

Never shampoo unless you have a wet-and-dry vacuum available.

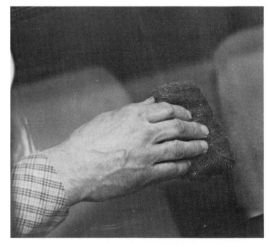

#00 steel wool or finer can be used to remove stubborn spots on glass. Use it with glass cleaner.

the cloth. Then wipe onto the vinyl. This method prevents overspray on surfaces you don't intend to dress, such as a dash with a combination of vinyl and metal parts.

In tight areas, use your finger as a guide. Feel along the ridge of a door panel so the dressing doesn't smear the glass. It also works well on dashes and center consoles.

On spots where your finger cannot fit, spray on the dressing directly. Use the cloth to remove excess. You may have to use just a corner or a fold of the cloth to reach it.

It is important to maintain a complete and even coverage when using dressing. A missed spot will stick out like a sore thumb. Take your time and concentrate on completeness.

Floor mats and foot pedals can be sprayed, and the excess wiped off. Dull-surfaced air vents can be dressed the same way. Vinyl woodgrain inserts on dashboards can also be dressed.

Clear lacquer

If you detailed the engine compartment, you probably used the clear lacquer. This paint can also be used on some areas inside some vehicles. You must exercise plenty of caution, however, to avoid unnecessary overspray.

Use a very light coat of clear lacquer on the vents. Too much paint will cause runs. These runs will be difficult to remove because the paint is sticky and you will be working in very tight spaces.

Pickup trucks with dark paint behind the seat are good candi-

Use your index finger inside the cloth as a guide
when dressing tight spots.

dates. The clear lacquer will enhance that area behind the seat and make it look fresh. The clear lacquer will also cover many slight scratches.

Doorjambs can be touched up with clear lacquer. It will make almost any painted surface look better. Use it on trunks, too. It brightens the paint and renews the shine it had when new.

Deodorizer

An interior usually smells quite clean after a detail. Not long after, though, the scent begins to fade. Use a pleasant-scented deodorizer to maintain the freshness. There is a wide variety available. Liquid kinds can be sprayed directly on carpets and under the front seat. Any type will do, even those designed for household use.

Another kind of deodorizer is solid. They usually come in the shape of small plastic trees, rainbows and so on. They can be hung from a knob or placed under the seat.

For vehicles with unusually heavy odor problems that persist even after a detail, try this: Place three or four of the plastic solid deodorizers under the front seat. Then, close all the windows and lock the car. Let it sit for three or four days. The scent will penetrate the carpet and upholstery. It should last for quite some time.

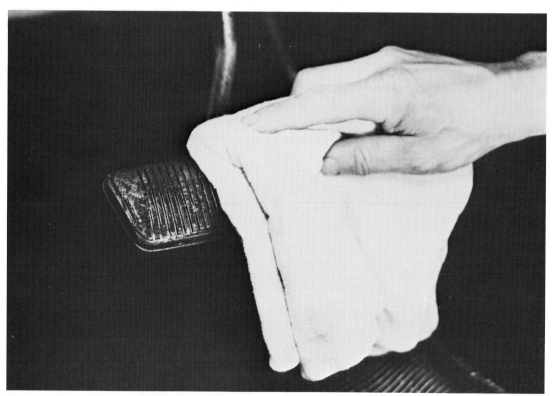

Remove excess dressing from foot pedals. Too much dressing may cause them to become slippery, a hazard when driving.

Chapter 8

Buffing

The term "buffing" refers to the procedure used to polish the paint on cars, boats, airplanes and almost any motor vehicle. Vehicles maintained with a good coat of wax seldom need to be buffed, because the paint remains in good shape. Buffing actually takes off a very thin layer of oxidized paint, exposing the good layers underneath.

Detailers have a wide range of waxes available for a number of different buffing jobs. It is almost impossible to recommend a particular wax without first seeing the car to be buffed. A "sealer" wax is most versatile. It contains very little cutter but will still remove slight oxidation. Rubbing compound is very gritty. It should never be applied with a buffer. Professional detailers mix different waxes to come up with special blends for unique jobs. The best advice I can give you is to try an over-the-counter liquid wax first. If it isn't strong enough to do the job, go to an automobile body and paint supply store and ask the salesperson to recommend a wax suited for the job you are doing.

When a car has not been waxed for an extended period, the paint fades. In severe cases, paint comes off the body and onto the wash mitt when it is washed. This means the top layer of paint is dead. It will not shine, no matter how much wax is put on. This kind of exterior has to be buffed or rubbed out by hand with rubbing compound.

Along with the oxidized paint, buffing also removes many slight

You can buff the paint on boats as well as cars and any other painted motor vehicles.

Using the buffer makes the job go much faster than rubbing out by hand.

scratches. If the scratches are deep and there is no paint under the scratch, the buffer has nothing to polish.

Other marks can also be removed by buffing. Soil deposits that have developed because of neglect and wet weather can be buffed out. Stains from fuel spillage can be buffed out as well. (These stains are most common at the bottom of the fuel tank inlet. As the fuel expands and fills the tank, it overflows out the inlet. This results in stains on the body. Washing will not remove them. Rubbing compound applied by hand and buffing will polish the paint in most cases.)

You do not have to use a buffer, however; the job can be done by hand. The machine simply makes the job easier and faster. If your car has oxidized paint, rub it out with rubbing compound. After that, use a regular wax to polish the good paint. Follow the directions on the can of rubbing compound for more precise instructions.

If you are in doubt about whether or not to buff, try hand waxing a small section of your car first. If the results are satisfactory, set aside a Saturday afternoon and hand wax it. If the results are poor, plan on renting a buffer.

Most over-the-counter waxes available at the auto parts store don't give specific information for machine use. That's why you should get the wax from a store that deals exclusively with automotive paint and polishing products. However, almost any liquid wax is all right to buff with. If it doesn't seem to do the job on the first try, buff again. Many times, weaker waxes will work very well the second time they are applied.

Hand rubbing

By far, the most physically demanding way to shine a car is by hand. The result will be equal to that of a buffer, but it will take much more time and elbow grease. Some people prefer to do it all by hand. There are detailers around who don't even own a buffer.

The type of wax to use depends on the amount and severity of oxidation. Rubbing compound is very potent; use it as a last resort. In general, use rubbing compound on special areas that need heavy rubbing to remove stains and paint marks such as those left by the doors of other cars.

Begin with a general wax and polish. See how it works. If it doesn't do the job, go to a wax with more cutter. Continue testing waxes until you find the one that works best.

Waxing by hand eliminates paint burns and body part damage. You will need to use a very soft cloth for application, such as diapers or towels. Follow the instructions on the label of the wax. Follow the same pattern as with a buffer: Always start at the highest point and work downward.

Some waxes come with an applicator sponge. You can use it, but remember, anything hard that is rubbed against the paint will create swirls. That's why most detailers use very soft cloths and waxes for their special cars.

If you need help choosing the best wax for your needs, ask the salespeople at the car-washing equipment and supply store or check with your local detail shop.

Cutting pad

The greatest hazard in buffing is burning the paint. There is no actual fire, but a spot of paint is totally removed down to the primer or the metal. This happens when the buffer is mishandled or is kept on one spot too long.

Always use the buffer in small sections at a time. Two square feet is a good section size. This will allow you to concentrate on your work and maintain complete control. Also, the wax won't have time to dry out, which causes spotting.

Ideally, the buffer should never rest in one place at all, ever. It should always be moving, or turned off. The speed of the pad and amount of cutter in the wax determines how much paint is removed. Also, the longer the pad rubs on a spot, the more paint is removed.

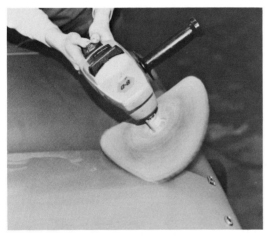

Unsafe handling of the buffer can cause paint burns or injury.

Buffing flat surfaces does not present the burning problems that ridges do.

Never rest the buffing pad directly on top of a ridge; you will surely burn the paint.

Buff up to the ridge with the edge of the buffing pad.

On flat surfaces such as roofs and hoods, paint burning is unlikely, except on the ridges. Use just the edge of the pad next to the ridge and throttle the buffer on and off to reduce the speed of the pad to help eliminate the chance of burning.

Use the ridge as a marking point. Buff a section above the ridge, then spread wax below it and buff. This way, you are always buffing up to the ridge, not on it.

After you buff a section, feel the paint. You will find it warm to the touch. The heat is due to the friction between the pad and the paint. This is why you cannot let the pad sit in one place while the buffer is on.

Use the ridges to set a buffing pattern. For example, a ridge in the center of the hood can divide the hood into two parts. Use the crack between the hood and the fender as another mark. Buff two square feet at a time between them until that side of the hood is done. Next, buff the top of the fender from the crack to the ridge on the corner of the fender. Buff up to the ridge and not on top of it. This so-called grid system helps to maintain an even pattern and ensures complete coverage.

You can do the same thing on the sides of the car. Use the bodyside moldings and cracks between the doors and body as your marking points.

Being right-handed, I like to start buffing at the hood on the driver's side. I buff in a counterclockwise direction, always moving to my right. It is easier to go to the right because my right arm is in a better position, especially when buffing the sides

While buffing the hood, the electrical cord will drag on top of the fender. Buffing that section last will remove any marks from the cord. To avoid possibly scratching the paint, drape the cord over your shoulder to keep it off the car.

On the hood, buff from the windshield toward the front of the car. Most hoods slant that way. When you come to a ridge, gently let the

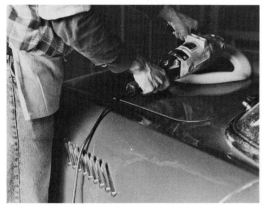

While buffing the hood or top, the buffer cord will rub against the fender or roof.

Drape the buffer cord over a shoulder.

edge of the pad buff the side of the ridge. Tilt the buffer slightly to facilitate movement of the machine. You don't have to raise it very high. You will have to practice with the buffer to get the feel for it. You can leave the buffer in one slanted position to buff. Go back and forth, from left to right, and toward and away from your body. Keep the machine moving.

Wax is thrown out from the buffer and can become quite messy. Every detail shop has wax spatter on the walls and floor after buffing. If you plan to buff inside your garage, use tarps or old sheets to cover anything you don't want spattered with wax.

Buff until the wax is gone. This ensures complete use of the wax sealers and glazes. After buffing a small section on the hood, use a soft cloth to remove any wax residue. Look at the buffed area. If it meets your aproval, move on. If it is still oxidized, you may have to buff it again. It could be that you didn't use enough wax the first time, or you went too fast, or the wax needed more cutter.

Cleaning the pad

While buffing, the pad will cake with wax. You should clean the pad at least four times during the job. If the job requires a lot of extra buffing, you may have to clean it more often. Clean the pad whenever it fails to pick up wax. Better yet, clean it before you start each new quarter.

Use a spur to clean the pad. If a pad spur is not available, carefully use a screwdriver. The spur is designed for cleaning pads. It removes wax with the least damage to the pad. Since pads are expensive, and because they can be used more than once, try to keep them in good condition by keeping them clean.

The teeth on the spur move freely. This enables them to remove wax and not damage the pad fibers. The screwdriver, on the other hand, is rigid. It will remove wax but may also tear the fibers.

Carefully rest the buffer on your leg. Be sure the cord is com-

Spread a small amount of wax on the car. Lay the buffer on the wax with low rpm. The lower speed will reduce wax spatter.

This is the hood of a 1967 Mustang after the car had been buffed. The spots are wax spatter.

pletely out of the way. With your left hand holding the handle, let your thumb depress the trigger. The buffer will have to be stabilized on your leg. The left hand must have a firm grip so that the torque does not spin it out of your hand.

The extension handle on the side of the buffer can rest against your other leg. You will start on the outer edge of the pad and work toward the middle. With the pad spinning, gently and slowly press the spur, or the screwdriver, into the pad. As the tool sinks into the pad, wax will be removed. (Dust and lint will come off the pad; you may want to wear eye protection.) Repeat the procedure two or three times. When you start to buff again, you'll notice how much easier it is working with a clean pad.

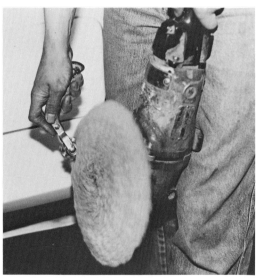

You can clean the pad with a spur.

Another method to clean the pad is with a screwdriver.

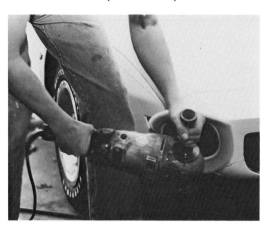

Rest your elbow on your leg. It makes the job easier and gives you more control.

Changing the position of your left hand makes buffing lower sections less awkward.

Front fender

Start at the top of each fender and work down. Use the ridges as a grid. To buff the sides, you will have to bend down. Spread the wax and buff between the ridge and the bodyside molding. You can rest your elbow on your leg while you buff. This gives more control and is easier on your back.

Buffing the bottom sections is awkward, but is accomplished by switching the position of your left hand. Rather than gripping the handle normally, grasp it with your thumb pointing away from the buffer. This allows more control of the buffer and ease of handling.

Bodyside moldings may come off when touched by the buffer. If the pad catches a small edge on the molding, the high revolutions will rip the molding off the car. (I know, it has happened to me, and probably every other detailer at least once.) It happens very quickly. Before you know it, the molding is off and laying on the floor a few feet away. So stay away from the moldings as much as possible. When you have to buff next to one, throttle the machine on and off to reduce the speed. Use the edge of the pad gently.

The cautions pertaining to the bodyside molding also hold true for letters and emblems on the car.

Don't go too fast with the buffer. You may be apprehensive about burning the paint, but going too fast will result in other problems. The "right" speed is difficult to define. The simplest explanation is to go at a pace that feels comfortable. An easy, relaxed speed is recommended. Move the buffer with authority, about as fast as you would move the wash mitt over the body.

Roof

Buff the roof after the front. Drape the cord over your shoulder to prevent it from dragging on the corner. Do a small section from front to rear, working toward yourself. If your rig sits high, like a 4x4, use a sturdy stool or ladder. Again, it is very important to do small sections

Use caution and throttle the buffer on and off when buffing around emblems and lettering.

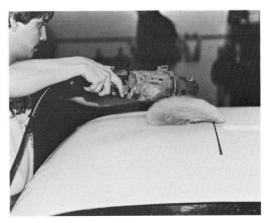

Buff the roof from front to rear and toward the edges.

at a time. This will keep your body in one position and stable, even when standing on the stool or ladder.

You can lean against the body for support. Make sure belt buckles and so on do not scratch the paint. If you do not have a heavy apron to use, move your belt buckle or remove the belt. Also avoid wearing pants with small metal rivets.

Doors, trunk and rear

When the roof is buffed, move to the front of the driver's door and continue buffing in an orderly manner, from top to bottom. When you reach the trunk, do the lid first and then each fender.

Difficult areas

The space around some door handles is hard to buff. Spread wax over the top and bottom of the handle. Then, with the buffer off, lay the pad on the area between the paint and the handle. Gently turn the buffer on and off, ensuring a slow speed. When the wax is gone, that area will be done.

Be sure to throttle the buffer on and off quickly. The pad should not reach full speed at any time. The slow speed of the pad will allow

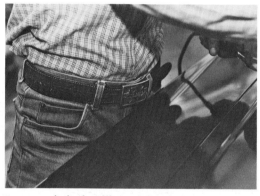

Remove belt buckles and other items from pants to avoid scratching.

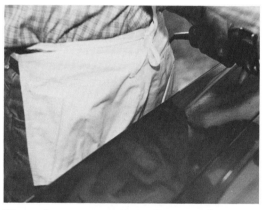

Wear a heavy apron to prevent scratches.

Buff the lower part of the door handle area. Throttle the buffer on and off for low rpm.

Position of the buffer and pad when buffing the top part of the door handle area.

the fibers to reach into the area and rub the paint. If fingernail scratches are still there after buffing, you will have to wax by hand to remove them.

The best procedure with some of these obstacles is to remove them before buffing. If your car has a power radio antenna, for example, lower it into its base and out of the way. If it is the screw-on type, take it off or shorten it. Push in the telescopic type as far as it will go.

Radio antennas have been ripped out of their sockets by buffers. Detailers have been smacked across the face by the whipping action of an antenna after the buffer hit it just right, so be careful.

Use the same basic procedure around antennas as with door handles. Squirt a little wax around the base. Then use the edge of the pad and throttle the buffer to maintain a slow speed. Work the buffer around the antenna. Only one side of the pad will be buffing. Be aware of the open side; it will be sticking up and may catch the antenna.

Windshield wiper blades pose the same problem as antennas. They too have been ripped off cars by the buffer. Use the edge of the pad and throttle the buffer. On imported cars, the wiper blades can be pulled away from the glass and put in a locked position.

With stationary wiper blades, you must work around them as best you can. Do not let the pad rub against the metal arms. This will cause the fibers of the pad to be pulled out, and it increases the chance of damaging the wiper.

If emblems are easily removed, take them off before buffing.

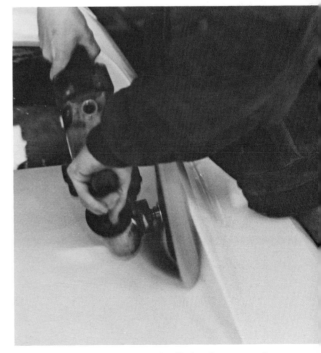

Throttle the buffer on and off for low speed when buffing in a difficult position or area.

Finishing pad

A finishing pad looks very much like the cutting pad, except it is much softer. Always use a very soft cream or liquid wax with it. The softness of the pad combined with the soft qualities of the wax will result in a deep, rich, scratch-free paint job.

Because the pad and the wax are so soft, paint burns are less likely. However, you can still burn the paint if you are careless. Follow the same general guidelines here as when using a cutting pad. Take the same precautions when you get near moldings or antennas.

Before buffing with the finishing pad, wipe off all the excess wax from the previous buffing. Any residual glaze or sealer wax may cause swirls, even with the finishing pad.

When using the finishing pad, you don't have to use much wax. Place a small dab on the car and buff it in. There will be very little wax spatter and little residue left on the car.

Chapter 9

Hand waxing

Even though you spent more time buffing, you must also apply a coat of protective wax. Not only will it help protect the layers of newly exposed paint, it also helps remove residual wax left behind by the buffer.

A cheap liquid wax works well to clean any mess left behind from buffing, but it will not last as long nor protect as well as a coat of high-quality carnuba wax. Carnuba protects the paint from sunlight, harsh weather and the normal hazards associated with driving.

Besides making a vehicle look its best, a coat of hand wax helps the car maintain its top-of-the-line resale value. First impressions are very important in the car world. Maintaining a car with a good wax job will command excellent first impressions.

Types of wax

There are so many kinds and brands of wax available that it is easy to become confused. Each claims to be the best, last the longest and apply the easiest.

Cream waxes are as easy to apply as any other. They seem to last longest, especially if they contain a lot of carnuba. Liquid waxes go on quickly but don't last nearly as long. The pastes last long enough, but are more susceptible to swirls. Read the labels and choose the one best suited to your needs.

When to wax

It is impossible to say just how long a wax job will last. It depends on a number of factors. Weather conditions play an important role. Will the vehicle be subjected to heavy rains, snow, ice and salted roads? Is the temperature exceptionally hot? Will the car or truck be parked outdoors in the hot sun every day? Or, will it stay in the garage except on Sundays?

Additional factors are frequency of washings and the type of soap used. The harsher the soap, the shorter the lifespan of the wax job. (It is best to use a very mild liquid dish soap to wash cars.)

The condition of the paint is also a consideration. If you wax an oxidized car, the wax will be absorbed by the layers of dead paint and not protect anything. I'm sure you have seen cars with large white blotches and streaks on them. They are the result of someone's attempt to merely wax an oxidized paint as opposed to buffing or rubbing out.

To determine how often your vehicle should be waxed, here is a rule of thumb: Whenever water fails to bead on the surface, wax it. Beading water is a sure sign of the presence of wax.

How to wax

Often, people in a hurry will wax only the top, hood and trunk lid. This is fine for a quick shine, but not after spending all day detailing.

Wax every painted part of the exterior. This includes spoilers, below the bumpers, around the grille, painted wheels and the chrome.

Most wax manufacturers suggest applying the wax sparingly. A heavy application wastes wax and is harder to remove. It is much better to apply a light coat, wipe it off and apply another light one, rather than to apply one heavy coat of wax.

The actual application of wax is rather simple: You wipe it on, and you wipe it off. If you faithfully use a certain routine, you will be guaranteed complete coverage the first time around.

Cautions

Of great importance is the danger of scratching, caused by rings and watches. If your hand should slide off the applicating cloth, you may put deep scratches in the paint.

As much as possible, avoid getting wax into cracks. Common trouble spots are between hood and fender, door and door post, and trunk lid and fender. Carelessness here just makes more work later on.

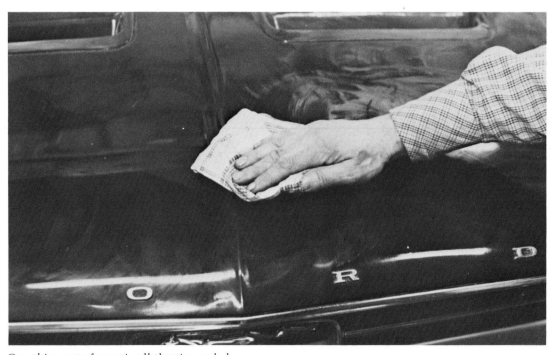

One thin coat of wax is all that is needed.

It is difficult to wax around emblems and letters without getting wax on them. Use your finger as a guide, as you did with the dressing.

Most wax instructions tell you to wax a small area and then wipe clean. I prefer to wax the whole car first. Then, while it is drying, I polish the chrome, dress the tires and do other finishing details, saving wax removal for last. Seldom are there any problems with the wax not coming off. You can try this on a small scale by waxing a small part of the body and letting it sit while you do something else. When you come back, wipe off the wax. If it comes off easily, you can go ahead and wax the entire car, then wipe it all off later, when you have completed other details.

Never wax a car in the sun. The sun will bake the wax into the paint and make it very difficult to remove. Waxing in cold temperatures is also a problem. Some waxes will not wipe off in cold weather, they will streak. Read the label on the wax to see what temperatures are recommended.

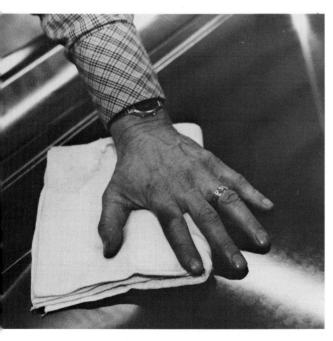

Remove rings and watches when rubbing on paint.

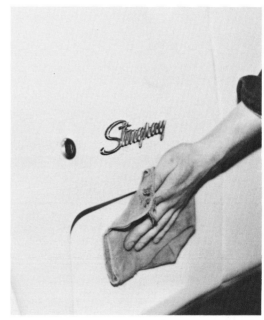

Start the hand wax away from cracks and emblems, then work the wax in toward them to reduce wax build-up.

Chapter 10

Exterior finishing

Painting

Fenderwell

Dirty fenderwells are an eyesore. Although not readily noticeable, they can be seen when viewing the car from the side, and especially on cars that have been jacked up. If you have detailed a rig to get a better selling price, a prospective buyer will most likely look at the tires and notice the fenderwells.

Paint the fenderwells with a glossy black paint. This is a must with 4x4s. Because they sit so high, the fenderwells are always plainly visible. Painting them will help set off and finish the rest of the vehicle. You will notice the improvement as soon as you start painting. The wheels will look shinier and the body paint, deeper.

Paint all of the easily seen areas of the well. You don't have to cover the very top or parts that are never noticed. Concentrate on the front and rear portions and the exposed area behind the wheel.

If overspray reaches the painted edge of the fenderwell, immediately use paint thinner to remove it. (If you leave hand wax on the car to dry, any residual overspray falling from the air will not touch

Painted fenderwell looks like new—clean and fresh.

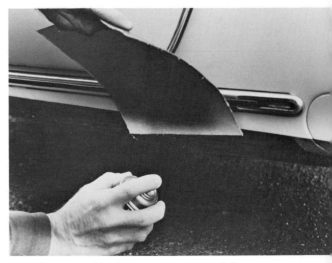

Use the paint block to paint exposed frame members below the rocker panels.

the paint.) When the job is done, it will look as if the car just went through an undercoating process. By the way, you can also buy undercoating material in a spray can. Instead of painting with black paint, you can give the fenderwells an undercoating.

Undercarriage

Along with the fenderwells, paint any visible undercarriage.

Below the rocker panels under the doors, you will see part of the main frame member running the length of the vehicle. By using a paint block, you can paint the frame that is exposed. Again, use glossy black. This makes a clean border between the painted body and the frame. It sets off the body and looks sharp and defined.

Don't go under the car to paint the bottom. Just paint the exposed members on the sides, front and rear.

Paint as much as possible at the rear end (especially on 4x4s). Paint not only the differential and axle, but the leaf springs, fuel tank, spare tire tread, trailer hitch brackets, frame and shocks. You can paint the shocks a different color; blue, yellow and white are the most common. Paint adds color and makes the shocks look new. Trailer-hitch parts under the bumper can be painted black. Those that stick out past the bumper can be painted bright silver or white.

Do the same for the front end. Especially on 4x4s, paint exposed frame members and steering linkages. You can also give a coat to cross-members, the bottom of the radiator and shocks. Watch for overspray on the bottom part of the engine.

You should not have to do much, if any, masking on the undercarriage. A paint block works fine; it's faster and easier to use, too. The edges of fenderwells will need no masking if you take your time and

Rear axle painted on a 4x4. Note the contrast made by the white shocks.

concentrate the paint on the exposed surface. Fancy shock absorbers can be protected by the paint block or a towel.

If you find yourself in a position to mask, use ordinary masking tape and newspaper. The supplies are easy to work with and are inexpensive. Do a thorough job when masking. Any slight flaw will be noticed.

Grille area

When doing paint work around the grille, use a width of masking tape that nearly covers the grille pieces by itself. This will free you from having to work with newspaper as a paint block. Such an example is when you have to paint the area behind the chrome grille. You can aim the nozzle between the grillework to coat the front of the radiator and other black metalwork.

Wheel

You can paint rims while they are on the car. Use the paint block on edge around the rim to protect the tire. Mask the valve stem. Keep the spray of the paint in line with the block. As you move around the wheel, keep the paint block in front of the paint. Overspray on the tire can be removed with thinner.

To paint the wheel white and the lug nuts black, you should remove the tire. For a quick touch-up on the white, you can mask the lugs and the valve stem. Always mask the valve stem—there is nothing that looks worse than a stem painted the same color as the wheel.

Painted silver wheels are commonly found on many imports. Use bright silver paint for them. Most wheels can be painted while still on the car. Remove the plastic covers from the lug nuts and hub. All you will have to mask is the valve stem, since the lugs and hub will be covered by the plastic caps after painting.

Tire

Tires do not need to be painted very often. A thorough scrubbing and dressing makes most tires look new. But, for badly stained tires and for blacking out whitewalls, you will need to use tire paint.

Tire paint is available at most auto parts stores. It is applied with a brush and generally takes more than one coat to black out a whitewall. Once you use it to cover whitewalls, you will have to do a touch-up again in a few months.

Snow tires and knobby motorcycle tires are difficult to paint. Use a small brush for hard-to-reach areas. A bigger brush can be used for the sidewalls. Have a rag handy to wipe the excess from the rim. The paint is rather thin and can run quite easily. Be sure to wait for the first coat to dry before applying the second coat.

Bumper

Most dock bumpers on trucks are painted. When repainting, use a glossy color. You can use any color, but silver and white are most common, although black is used as well. If you are thinking about using black, remember that you will already have painted much of the lower rear end area that color—too much black doesn't always look good.

Tailgate

Use the paint block to prevent overspray on the tailgate. You can also drape towels over body parts for protection. Remove the license plate or carefully use the paint block over it. Mask any small identification tags on the bumper, as well as license plate lights. Thinner can be used on the lights and plates to remove any overspray. Don't paint over the manufacturer tags.

Floor mat and trunk carpet

Black floor mats often get scratched and fade. You can paint them with black glossy lacquer. You must apply the paint lightly and allow plenty of time for it to dry before adding a second coat. The paint will not last long, however. This is more of a quick-fix touch-up rather than a long-term solution.

Black trunk mats and carpet can also be sprayed with a light coat of black paint. The thin carpet in trunks is difficult to get perfectly clean and free of lint. Wear spots are also a problem.

Remove the carpet from the trunk before you apply a very thin coat of paint. The thin coat will cover stains and wear spots. Too heavy an application will cause the paint to cake, making the carpet brittle. It will also look bad.

You don't have to paint the entire carpet, just cover the worn spot. Be sure to allow plenty of time for the paint to dry before replacing the carpet.

Interior

Shift levers, especially those on the floor, often get wear spots. You can paint them with a high-gloss paint.

Valve stem should have been masked. Tire needs new coat of paint to cover old whitewall.

#00 steel wool and wax is used to shine the chrome on this headlight ring for a 1968 Porsche.

Touch-up paints are available at most auto parts stores. They come in small glass bottles and spray cans in many colors. To apply paint from a bottle to a paint chip, dab with the unburned end of a paper match. When using the spray, the paint block and/or towels will prevent overspray.

The exposed seat brackets on pickup trucks get wear spots from seat belts and feet. When painting them, use the paint block and towels. If needed, use masking tape next to the bracket and on the painted floor to guard against overspray. Towels work very well to protect the seat from overspray.

Polishing
Chrome

Chrome cleaners and polishes work very well, but a less expensive method is to use #00 steel wool and wax. The steel wool removes blemishes and the wax acts as a polisher and protectant. Don't use steel wool coarser than #00, it may scratch.

Spread a little wax on the pad of steel wool. Then vigorously polish the chrome. Some wax will remain on the chrome and will have to be wiped off later. Use this method on all chrome, including bumpers, mirrors, brightwork, door handles, fender moldings, light rings and hood ornaments.

Steel wool and wax can also be used to shine radio antennas, wheels, hubcaps, engine parts, and even pieces on the dash.

Dressing
Exterior

The same multipurpose dressing used for the interior can be used on the exterior of the vehicle. Before dressing, make sure the part is dry. For tires, spray the dressing on and then wipe off the excess with a clean towel. Cover all of the rubber with a uniform spray. The tire will look new again. Be sure to wipe off any excess from the wheel and the tire. If you don't, the dressing may streak.

All exterior rubber and vinyl surfaces should be dressed. Spray dressing on a cloth and apply to bodyside moldings, door moldings, weather stripping, mud flaps, bumper guards and even the woodgrain vinyl designs on station wagons. Excess dressing on chrome or paint can be wiped off with a clean cloth.

Vinyl top

Multipurpose dressing can be used on vinyl tops. The top must be clean before application. If you buffed the paint, there may be wax and lint on the vinyl. Use a damp cloth to wipe it off. You may have to do this more than once. (Turn the cloth over and unfold as necessary, as a side gets soiled.)

You can carefully spray the dressing directly on the top or spray it on a cloth first and then apply. Either way you must work in the dressing with a clean cloth. You will see the difference right away, especially on dark vinyls. Dressing will enhance the beauty of the vinyl, giving it a soft and shiny appearance.

If the vinyl is severely dry and hasn't been dressed for quite some time, the multipurpose dressing may not work as well as you hoped. In that case, you can apply a dressing specifically made for vinyl tops.

Vinyl top dressing is sold at auto parts stores. It is a clear, sticky fluid designed to rejuvenate vinyl tops and protect them with a hard shell. It is recommended to pour the dressing on a cloth and then apply to the vinyl.

The very sticky nature of the vinyl top dressing requires special clean-up. Follow the manufacturer's recommendations on the label.

The lasting quality of vinyl top dressing is much better than multipurpose dressing, but it will not last forever. As with the wax job, its longevity will depend on weather and washing factors.

Uniform application of the dressing is a must. Any spots missed will be easily recognized. Apply two coats if necessary.

Dressing on the chrome strips around the vinyl can be removed after it has hardened. Use #00 steel wool. For other excesses, follow the instructions on the dressing label.

If the vinyl top on your car doesn't clean up as well as you think it should, or if you have another problem with it, don't dress it. First, seek the advice of a vinyl top installer or detailer. They can help determine what it will take to thoroughly clean the top or advise you

Apply tire dressing and wipe off the excess.

Excess dressing should have been wiped off. Note the streaks.

on how to solve a specific problem. If you use the vinyl top dressing on a top that needs repair or subsequent cleaning, the work will be much harder to do.

Dyeing
Vinyl top
Some vinyl tops are so neglected that no amount of cleaning or dressing will bring them back to life. In those instances, you will have to dye the vinyl.

Special dyes are made for vinyl tops. Many brands and colors are available at auto body equipment and supply stores. Read the labels for the specific qualities of each brand and the directions for application.

Vinyl top dyes come in different application types. Some are put on with a spray gun, others with a sponge brush. Before using either type you must clean the vinyl according to the instructions on the label. Mask off all of the strips that border the vinyl, including window edges. You should also lay clean towels over the windshield, hood and trunk, just in case any dye is kicked up by the applicating brush. Also be aware of belt buckles and rivets on jeans. While applying the dye you will be leaning against the car. Don't make the mistake of scratching the paint while beautifying the top!

The application of dye is much like painting. If you use a spray, be cautious to avoid overspray. Cover any part of the car that you think might be vulnerable to it. If you use the brush, set the dye on the vinyl when you dip the brush for more dye. This way, you won't have to worry about dripping dye on the body of the car.

Rear seat deck
Vinyl top dye can also be used to color the deck above and behind the back seat at the base of the rear window. This ledge is exposed to a lot of sunlight and often fades. Dye could be the solution for making it look new again.

Because of the slant of the rear window, it may be very difficult to dye. It is best to practice first with a clean brush. The configuration of the rear window combined with the shape of the side walls may make dyeing much too difficult. If that is the case, you can cut a piece of carpet to fit, instead.

The procedure for dyeing the deck is the same as for the top. Be sure to cover the seats. Take your time, you will be working in close quarters.

Interior
All of the interior of a vehicle can be dyed. There are spray cans of dye available for that purpose. Dyeing the seats, door panels, headliner and dash is a major job. Masking will have to be done, and other precautions need to be taken. To do an extensive dye job, you should take the seats out of the car and remove all chrome strips and knobs. Overspray will be a problem, not only on dash parts but also on glass.

Before you decide to dye the entire interior of your car, consider the alternatives and get advice from experts. If the upholstery is beginning to wear, you will have to re-cover soon anyway. The same holds true for the headliner. But if just one door panel looks bad, you can probably find an identical panel in good shape at a wrecking yard.

Cleaning
Windows

For stubborn spots and overspray on windows, you can use #00 steel wool with the soap spray. The steel wool works very well to remove bugs and other things that stick to glass. Spray the glass, rub with steel wool, then pick up the moisture with the towel.

Some glass is severely stained with water spots. Try steel wool first. If it doesn't work, you can try buffing with the buffer and wax. However, buffing doesn't work every time, either. Some parts of the country have extremely hard water. The water dries on the glass and is almost impossible to remove. If you come across a problem such as this, go to a glass shop for advice.

If you plan to buff the paint, save the glass cleaning for last. Buffing will spatter wax on the windows. It is unnecessary to clean the glass until all other detailing is done.

When the entire vehicle is detailed, you should drive it into the sunshine for a final check. The bright sunlight will quickly reveal any streaks or smears left on the glass.

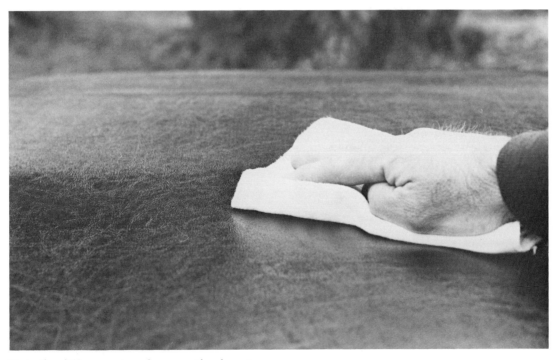

Note the difference in color once the dressing has been applied to the vinyl roof.

Chapter 11

Final wipedown

If you have done a complete detail, the windows will be dirty. Clean them now using the method described earlier.

The vehicle will then be sitting with clean windows, dressed vinyl and rubber, painted fenderwells and undercarriage—and wax all over the body and chrome.

To wipe off the wax, you will need at least two clean, soft towels, or cheesecloths. Fold the towel or cheesecloth into quarters so you will have a number of different sides to use. You should initially wipe a section with one side and then go over it again with a clean side to pick up any residual wax and streaks. Never use a cloth that has been used for something else, and don't let a side get so caked with wax that it won't pick up any more.

Wipe off the body before the chrome. There may be fibers of steel wool on the chrome and you wouldn't want to rub them into the paint.

The pattern is the same as for the rest of the detailing. Start at the hood and work around the car doing the top and then the sides.

Every wax job results in some wax getting into cracks and crevices, no matter how careful you are. The buffer is a major cause of this.

Use the nylon brush to remove wax build-up around hood scoop.

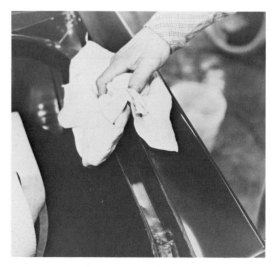

Remove wax from the trunk edges with a soft cloth.

When the body has been wiped down, open the doors, hood and trunk and wipe off any wax on the edges.

For removing wax build-up near emblems and lettering, use the one-inch-wide paint brush (with the bristles cut off to about three quarters of an inch). Getting rid of all the wax build-up greatly improves the overall appearance of the buffing and waxing. Use the brush along seams and inside parts of emblems. Many times, it will appear that the black background paint on an emblem is chipped. But after you use the cut-off brush on it, you will notice that what you thought were chips was actually wax build-up.

Use the brush around the windshield wipers, radio antennas, moldings, louvers, door handles, window moldings, brightwork and carriage bolts on the bumpers.

Nylon brush works well to remove wax in louvers.

Clean wax spatter off windshield wipers with a cloth and nylon brush.

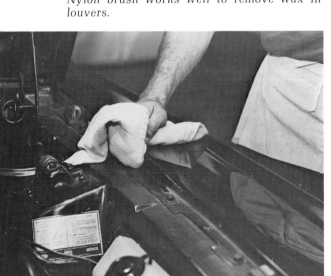

Remove wax from the edge around the hood. Notice the apron the detailer is wearing.

Remove wax from the trunk lid.

When the body has been completed, wipe off the chrome. Wipe off headlights and parking lamps, using the brush as needed. Then walk around the car and check for missed wax. Recheck doors, hood and trunk.

When all of that is done, drive the rig outside and park it in the sunlight. This is the final inspection. Right away, some things may be very obvious—a spot missed when dressing the tire, a streak or smear on a window, or a spot where the wax was not wiped off. This is the time to go over the vehicle with a fine-tooth comb.

The following is a checklist of things you should look for when the car is parked in the sun.

    1) body, missed wax
    2) windows, smears and streaks
    3) paint, flaws on fenderwells and undercarriage
    4) tires, dressing
    5) chrome, missed wax
    6) engine, paint flaws
    7) hood edge, wax

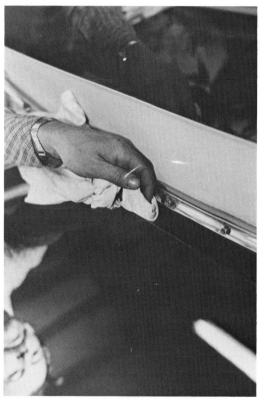

Remove wax from the front part of the trunk lid, next to the white convertible top. Note the detailer's reflection on the freshly buffed and waxed trunk lid.

A solid-style deodorizer.

8) interior, lint and dressing coverage

9) trunk, lint and wax

10) emblems and keyholes, wax

11) doorjambs, wax

Then, replace all the things you took out of the trunk and glove compartment. With all of that done, your automobile should look the best it has looked in years. Every part of it was detailed except for the very bottom of the undercarriage. There shouldn't be a speck of dirt or dust anywhere on it. All of the vinyl has been dressed and all the paint waxed. The very last thing to do is spray a bit of deodorizer on the carpets or hang a solid deodorizer from a knob. Now your car, truck, motorhome, motorcycle or boat looks, feels and smells like new. Sit down and admire it.

The beautiful wax shine of the trunk section of a classic 1957 T-Bird. What a difference a detail makes!

Appendix

Engine compartment painting

The engine should be hot from idling before you begin to paint. The high temperature makes the paint dry quickly and helps reduce runs. Be very careful when working around it. If you have to rest your arm on the radiator to reach a part of the engine, lay a heavy towel on it first.

Dry excess water

A long engine idle may not evaporate all the water from cleaning. Pockets can still remain on top of the intake manifold and air cleaner. The easiest way to get rid of water is to soak it up with a towel. You can also use air from a compressor, a blow dryer or a wet-and-dry vacuum. When the air cleaner housing is dry, remove it. This will give you access to the manifold.

Final engine cleaning

When the engine compartment is dry, you may notice some spots that were missed while cleaning. Most obvious will be black inner fenderwells. When wet, they look clean. When dry they show the streaks. Use a damp towel to clean them.

Look around the engine compartment for other dirty spots. This is the last chance you'll have to clean before you start painting. A rag with a dab of solvent works nicely on most greasy spots. Check the compartment thoroughly.

Use a wet-and-dry vacuum hose to remove water from the intake manifold.

Top of engine and carburetor were not cleaned completely because the air cleaner was not removed. Paint flaking on valve cover can be taken off with high-pressure water.

Air cleaner

Paint the air cleaner first, while it is still warm, using glossy black paint. Do the painting where overspray will not be a problem. You can lay newspapers on the floor and set the cleaner on top of a coffee can. This enables you to paint the bottom, sides and top all at once, without having to lift it up and move it around.

Hold the air cleaner by the spout. Tip it upside down and paint the bottom. When the bottom is done, lay it upright on the can and paint the top. Any small marks left on the bottom by the coffee can will not be seen once the air cleaner is on the carburetor.

Painting the sides of the air cleaner poses no problems. Follow the instructions on the can of spray paint. Hold the can away from the surface as recommended. The paint should apply evenly with few runs.

Labels and stickers on the air cleaner should not be painted. These stickers often list the size of the engine or contain other pertinent information. Painting over them looks cheap and unprofessional. You can carefully cover them with masking tape before you paint. Or you can be ready to clean them with a rag and paint thinner as soon as they're painted. Never use lacquer thinner. It is much too strong and will remove the writing from the stickers. Using paint thinner takes longer but will not remove the lettering. Use just enough to remove the overspray.

The wing nut used to hold the air-cleaner housing should be painted bright silver. When you paint the wing nut, also paint the inside of the metal ashtrays and the radiator cap. Most import cars have a dark brown plastic ashtray. After cleaning, they can be painted with clear lacquer.

Chrome air cleaners can be cleaned and polished later. This will give you time to paint the engine while it is still warm.

Air cleaners on certain imports may be painted the same color as

Set the air-cleaner housing on a coffee can to paint. Newspapers catch overspray.

Plastic ashtray painted with clear lacquer. Air cleaner wing nut, radiator cap and half of a metal ashtray painted with bright silver.

the engine compartment or a different color. If it really needs a coat of paint, and you don't have stock paint, use glossy black or bright silver. Otherwise, just clean it and then paint with clear lacquer.

Valve cover caps

Remove oil filler caps as well as the cap which holds the hose from the air cleaner. They are easiest to paint while out of the car and on a workbench or lying on newspapers on the floor. Paint them the stock color. If they are chrome, polish them when you do the chrome air cleaner.

After painting, leave them to dry. Return to the engine and wipe up any oil that may have spilled on the valve covers.

Engine

To paint the engine, you'll need the correct color and type of engine paint, a paint block, rags and lacquer thinner.

Use a systematic approach to engine painting. Start at the front. Paint everything that can be reached from that point, using the paint block to cover the carburetor, fan belts and so on. At times, you may have to use a stool to reach lower areas (a five-gallon bucket turned upside down makes a good one).

For hard-to-reach areas, such as the bottom of the block, you will have to be on your toes. Make sure your index finger is properly positioned on the nozzle of the paint can. A good rule of thumb is to place the opening of the nozzle in line with the direction your finger is pointing. This way, you always know where the paint is going to spray. Use short bursts of spray. Holding the can too long on one spot will cause runs in the paint.

You may have to use your thumb to activate the nozzle; for instance, at the bottom of the block. There is no way to hold the can in the normal manner. Be imaginative. Operate the paint spray any way you deem necessary to achieve a good paint job.

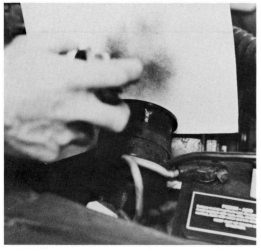

Use the paint block while painting a part black.

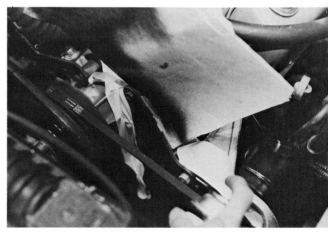

Use the paint block and masking tape while painting the bracket for the power steering unit.

If one light coat of paint does not provide adequate coverage, let it dry before applying a second coat. These paints normally dry quickly. The warm engine also speeds it.

It is a good idea to recheck your paint work after the entire engine has had one coat. This affords plenty of time for the paint to dry so you can start the second coat immediately. It also gives you the chance to paint any spots missed the first time around.

Obstructions

Don't be afraid to move parts out of the way. The biggest obstructions are hoses and wires. Use your hand to pick up and hold wires and hoses while the other hand paints under them. Remove wires from their holding clips if necessary. You may have to wipe them down to remove overspray. Use the paint block and rags anywhere you think they can help.

Spark plugs and ignition wires will be in the way, too. You can maneuver around them. Or, you can remove each plug and wire one by

Keep your finger in line with the nozzle opening of the paint can. Wherever your finger points, the paint will spray.

This spot on the intake manifold next to GM was missed during initial painting.

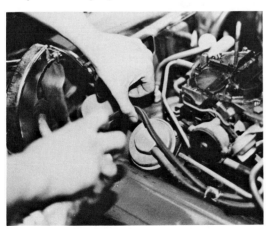

Move vacuum lines out of the way while painting the valve cover.

Remove as many obstacles as possible when painting the engine.

one, paint, and then replace. This ensures that they stay in their correct order. (The vehicle will run very rough, if at all, if the firing order of the plugs is not correct.) This method is probably the safest way to paint around the plugs—you get adequate coverage with no overspray.

Another way is to use a small section of garden hose that will fit over the spark plug while you paint. (Make sure the hose diameter is big enough.) Remove the wires one by one and replace them after each area is painted. Having only one wire off at a time ensures they are put back where they belong.

Use the paint block or a rag to protect exhaust manifolds. Overspray is removed with lacquer thinner. Any remaining overspray will quickly burn off the first time the engine is warmed up.

When painting the top of the intake manifold, to get good coverage, you may have to remove some small parts, such as the throttle return spring, air cleaner hoses, vacuum hoses and plastic clips for the ignition wires. Remove these one at a time, also.

Paint every part of the engine that was painted at the factory, including water pump, thermostat, cam chain housing and visible bell housing. The emphasis is on doing a thorough job. Try to avoid overspray, but don't be too meticulous—overspray will come off.

To check your work, use a drop light. Determine areas that were missed and any that need a second coat. (Working in a garage or shop doesn't always afford the greatest light under the hood. A drop light is a must. It is a good idea to use one in the engine compartment while you are painting. A good place to hang one is from the hood. You can also lay it down near your work.)

If you are detailing a 4x4 or other rig where the oil pan is visible from outside the engine compartment, paint it. You will have to paint from under the vehicle. Use the paint block and rags to prevent overspray.

Black areas

Fresh paint on the black areas of the engine compartment will help show off the engine. These areas are fenderwells (if they are already black), steering box, brake fluid reservoir, radiator and so forth. Glossy black lacquer works the best. The shiny results add to the entire detail job.

Start at the bottom of the compartment and work up. (This way, you won't have to worry about resting your elbow on wet paint.) Use the paint block as necessary. Spray the paint lightly; don't try to cover everything with one heavy coat. Two light coats result in a much better job.

Frame members at the bottom of the compartment almost always need a coat of paint. Hold wires out of the way and paint. Brake lines can be quickly wiped off if paint gets on them. Use the paint block to protect other hoses and lines.

Firewalls can be painted too. On most cars, they are the same color as the rest of the car. Here, use clear lacquer. Remember to use plenty of rags to prevent overspray. Drape them over the bell housing and cover the painted body next to the windshield. Use masking tape to hold them in place.

This painting process is slow and methodical. Use a light touch on the spray paint. The engine will have cooled, so runs are more apt to appear.

The body of the brake fluid reservoir should be painted black, but the cap can be painted silver or gold. It is easiest to remove the cap and paint it with the ashtrays and air-cleaner housing. Bright silver looks very nice.

When painting, always be cautious about overspray or spillage on the body. Use plenty of towels. Lay them across the fenders while you work under the hood. This protects the fenders from scratches as well as paint drops.

The radiator is next to paint. You will have leaned against it many times while painting other parts of the engine compartment. Be sure to paint each side as well as the top. If the front or back of the radiator also needs painting, by all means paint it.

Hood underbody

Once again, if this area is not black and is not in need of paint, don't paint it. But, if the original paint is just about gone or the black paint is in need of a face lift, paint it.

There are several precautions you must take before painting the hood underbody. There will be quite a bit of overspray. Some of it will come off the fenders when they are buffed. But if the vehicle has had a recent paint job, you must cover the fenders, cowling, windshield

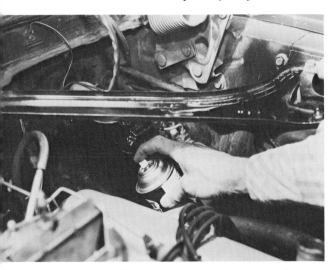

Paint the firewall. Note the position of the noz-zle and finger.

Use a spray gun to paint black engine com-partment areas. Note the drop of black paint on the fender under the spray gun.

and roof. Large towels work fine. You should drape a couple of towels over the engine, too.

Use a clean paint block to outline the outer edges of the hood. (Any wet paint remaining on a used block will rub off and smear the hood.) Paint the hood in sections. Start at the back of one side and work forward.

Long strokes can be used when painting the center of the hood. Along the edges, use short strokes and stay within the limits of the paint block. Continue painting until one side is done. Then move to the other side.

Slight overspray spots can be removed with paint thinner. Do not use lacquer thinner; it can remove old paint along with the overspray.

Removing overspray

The single most important factor in engine detailing is cleanup. Getting rid of every speck of paint overspray gives the engine a new face and shows the professionalism of the detailer. It allows the various colors to show. The very last thing you want is for the engine to look as if you covered the carburetor and then dipped the engine and accessories into a big bucket of paint.

Use enough lacquer thinner to wet a spot about two inches in diameter on a rag. Place that part of the rag between your thumb and index finger. Wipe all of the wires along the intake manifold, and those on the firewall and fenderwells. Then do the hoses, clamps, plugs, springs, linkages, filters, carburetor, distributor, coil, fuel pump and so on. You will have to stick your head into the engine compartment and use a drop light to find all of the parts with overspray. This is a meticulous job, but the work will pay off.

To get overspray off the exhaust manifolds, you'll have to dab a bit of thinner on a rag and rub. If all the overspray doesn't come off, it will be sufficiently dulled so that the first time the engine is run the heat will burn it off.

Overspray on painted surfaces can be removed with rubbing compound. Most of the time, it comes off very easily. Don't use lacquer thinner, though. It will ruin the good paint underneath. Lacquer will also ruin stickers and labels.

When you think all of the overspray is gone and everything is painted to perfection, stop, take a break and get something cold to drink. When you are ready to get back to work, get the drop light and check your work one more time. Repaint anything that needs it and remove any overspray you find.

Finally, replace all of the parts you took off except the chrome ones. Check the carburetor linkages to make sure they are in position. See that the ignition wires fit snugly in place on the spark plugs. Open the distributor and check for moisture on the cap.

Clear lacquer and dressing

In addition to a perfect job of removing overspray, clear lacquer is one of the best things around for engine detailing. It makes everything shine like it did on the showroom floor. It also covers many dirty spots on hoses and dark paint.

Before painting, cover the fenders, windshield and cowling. There will be a lot of overspray because virtually everything under the hood will be painted.

Systematically start at one end of the firewall. Paint the lowest parts first. Work your way up the firewall until it is covered. Then do the back of the engine up to the manifold. Move toward the front, painting the lowest parts first. Work around the compartment until everything is covered. Paint the bottom sides of hoses, accessories and wires. Paint the bottom of the air cleaner, too.

The space between the radiator and grille is often missed, so are the sides of the radiator. Do a small section at a time to ensure complete coverage. After the sides, front and rear are done, use long, sweeping strokes to cover the entire top of the engine including the inner fenderwells. Stop spraying each time you reach the end of a sweep. You will be using a start-go method—spray, stop, reverse direction and spray again.

Next to the radiator are the horn units and headlight housings. Spray them, too. Also spray the plastic containers for the radiator overflow and the windshield washer fluid. After just a few strokes you will see what a difference clear lacquer makes. Everything will shine like new and the dirty spots will disappear. Take your time, let the spray settle and recheck your work.

The last thing to paint with clear lacquer is the hood. Make sure the towels are in place to catch any overspray. Use long, even strokes. You will be able to see the kind of coverage you are getting. The end result will be a hood that looks like it was just completely repainted.

When all of the clear painting is done, you can replace the chrome parts that were removed earlier.

If you are detailing an expensive show car or a foreign exotic, you may elect not to use clear lacquer on the engine. If that is the case, you can get much the same results from dressing.

The black overspray on the label for the air-conditioning unit must be carefully removed.

289 V-8 engine in a 1967 Mustang convertible, completely detailed.

Squirt dressing on a cloth and then rub it into the hoses and wires. Do not spray it directly on the parts. The overspray will not look good. The dressing will not cover water spots on paint or stains. It makes hoses and wires look new. This process will take more time but is preferred by some car owners.

Both clear lacquer and dressing will make the engine compartment look new. Neither one will last forever. The clear lacquer will eventually fade and the dressing will dry out. The choice is yours. Either way, you will have an engine compartment that looks like it is fresh from the factory.

Special tip

Painting engines is not new. However, detailers are always looking for ways to do the job better and faster. One good tip is to use the plastic tube from a can of WD-40 to paint in very tight places. Be sure the nozzle on the paint can will accept the tube (not all of them will). This extends the reach of the paint and eliminates a lot of overspray.

If you have an idea that may make the job easier or quicker, by all means try it. But always take the necessary precautions. You can never have too many rags covering a part to prevent overspray, and you will hardly ever go wrong if you follow the directions on the products you use.

The plastic tube from a can of WD-40 can be used to apply engine paint in a tight spot.